Allyn and Bacon

Criminal Justice on the Net

2002 Edition

Thomas R. O'Connor
North Carolina Wesleyan

Allyn and Bacon
Boston • London • Toronto • Sydney • Tokyo • Singapore

NOTICE: Between the time Web site information is gathered and then published, it is not unusual for some sites to have ceased operating. Also, the transcription of URLs can result in unintended typographical errors. The Publisher would appreciate notification where these occcur so that they may be corrected in subsequent editions. Thank you.

In its effort to provide a diverse list of Web sites, the Publisher has included links that do not necessarily represent the views of Allyn and Bacon. Faculty, students, and researchers are strongly advised to use their analytical skills to determine the truth, accuracy, and value of the content in individual Web sites.

TRADEMARK CREDITS: Where information was available, trademarks and registered trademarks are indicated below. When detailed information was not available, the publisher has indicated trademark status with an initial capital where those names appear in the text.

Macintosh is a registered trademark of Apple Computer, Inc.

Microsoft is a registered trademark of Microsoft Corporation. Windows, Windows95, Windows98, and Microsoft Internet Explorer are trademarks of Microsoft Corporation.

Netscape and the Netscape Communicator logo are registered trademarks of Netscape Communications Corporation.

Contents

Part 2   Activities in Criminology and Criminal Justice

Part 3   Documentation

Glossary   135

1

Introduction
to the Internet

You're about to embark on an exciting experience as you become one of the millions of citizens of the Internet. Once you've accustomed yourself to this wonderful new world, you'll be amazed by how much you can discover, learn, and accomplish as you explore the Internet's dynamic resources.

Why Use the Internet?

In *Understanding Media,* Marshall McLuhan foresaw the existence of the Internet when he described electronic media as an extension of our central nervous system. On the other hand, today's students introduced to the Internet for the first time describe it as "cool."

No matter which description you favor, you are immersed in a period that is transforming the way we live by transforming the nature of the information we live by. As recently as 1980, intelligence was marked by "knowing things." If you were born in that year, by the time you were old enough to cross the street by yourself, that definition had changed radically. Today, in a revolution that makes McLuhan's vision tangible, events, facts, rumors, and gossip are distributed instantly to all parts of the global body. The effects are equivalent to a shot of electronic adrenaline. No longer the domain of the privileged few, information is shared by all the inhabitants of McLuhan's global village. Meanwhile, the concept of information as intelligence feels as archaic as a television remote control with a wire on it (ask your parents about that).

With hardly more effort than it takes to rub your eyes open in the morning, you can connect with the latest news, gossip about your favorite music group or TV star, learn the best places to eat on spring break, find out the weather back home, or follow the trials and tribulations of that soap opera character whose life conflicts with your history class. You can carry on a real-time conversation with your best friend at a college half a continent away, or play interactive games with a dozen or more world-wide challengers. And that's just for fun. When it comes to your education, newspaper and magazine archives are now almost instantly available, as are the contents of many reference books. Distant and seemingly unapproachable experts are found answering questions in discussion groups or electronic newsletters.

The Internet also addresses the major problem facing us in our split-second, efficiency-rated culture: Where do we find the time? The Internet allows professors and students to keep in touch, collaborate, and learn without placing unreasonable demands on individual schedules. Professors are posting everything from course syllabi to homework solutions and are increasingly answering questions online, all in an effort to ease the pressure for face-to-face meetings by supplementing them with cyberspace offices. The Internet enables students and professors to expand office hours into a twenty-four-hours-a-day, seven-days-a-week operation. Many classes have individual sites at which enrolled students can gather electronically to swap theories, ideas, resources, gripes, and triumphs.

By freeing us from the more mundane operations of information gathering, and by providing numerous diverse sources of information, the Internet encourages us to be more creative and imaginative. Instead of devoting most of our time to gathering information and precious little to analyzing and synthesizing it, the Internet tips the balance in favor of the skills that separate us from silicon chips. As much as the Internet ties us together, it simultaneously emphasizes our individual skills—our ability to connect information in new, meaningful, and exciting ways. Rarely have we had the opportunity to make connections and observations on such a wide range of topics, to create more individual belief systems, and to chart a path through learning that makes information personally useful and meaningful.

A Brief History of the Internet

The Internet began as a tool for national defense. In the mid-1960s, the U.S. Department of Defense was searching for an information analogy to the new Interstate Highway System, a way to move computing resources around the country in the event the Cold War caught fire. The immediate predicament, however, had to do with the Defense Department's budget, and the millions of dollars spent on computer research at universities and think tanks. Much of these millions was spent on acquiring, building, or modifying large computer systems to meet the demands of the emerging fields of computer graphics, artificial intelligence, and multiprocessing (where one computer was shared among dozens of different tasks).

While the research was distributed across the country, the unwieldy, often temperamental, computers were not. This made it difficult for computer scientists at various institutions to share their work without duplicating each other's hardware. Wary of being accused of re-inventing the wheel, the Advanced Research Projects Agency (ARPA), the funding arm of the Defense Department, invested in the ARPANET, a private network that would allow disparate computer systems to communicate with each other. Researchers could remain among their colleagues at their home campuses while using computing resources at government research sites thousands of miles away.

A small group of ARPANET citizens soon began writing computer programs to perform little tasks across the Internet. Most of these programs, while ostensibly meeting immediate research needs, were written for the challenge of writing them. These programmers, for example, created the first email systems. They also created games such as "Space Wars" and "Adventure." Driven in large part by the novelty and practicality of email, businesses and institutions accepting government research funds begged and borrowed their way onto the ARPANET, and the number of connections swelled.

As the innocence of the 1960s gave way to the business sense of the 1980s, the government eased out of the networking business, turning the ARPANET (now Internet) over to its users. While we capitalize the word "Internet," it may surprise you to learn there is no "Internet, Inc." in charge of this uniquely postmodern creation. Administration of this world-wide communication complex is still handled by the cooperating institutions and regional networks that comprise the Internet. The word "Internet" denotes a specific interconnected network of networks, not a corporate entity.

The emergence of the World Wide Web, developed by the European Laboratory for Particle Physics in the early 1990s, transformed the Internet. For the first time, images as well as text could be viewed through the aid of graphical Web browsers (software for navigating the Web).

part
1

Today, sophisticated browsers such as Netscape Navigator and Microsoft Internet Explorer have led to the Web's vast popularity.

Some Things You Ought to Know

In order to access the Internet, you must first have an Internet Service Provider (ISP). That's the organization providing you with your Internet account. Most of the time your ISP will be your school; but you may contract with one of the commercial providers such as America Online, the Microsoft Network, Earthlink, or AT&T.

Much of the confusion over the Internet comes from two sources. One is terminology. Just as the career you're preparing for has its own special vocabulary, so does the Internet. You'd be hard pressed to join in the shoptalk of archeologists, librarians, or carpenters if you didn't speak their language. Don't expect to plop yourself down in the middle of the Internet without some buzzwords under your belt, either. This chapter will explain the most common terms, but keep in mind that new Internet technologies are developing all the time.

The second source of confusion is that there are often many ways to accomplish the same ends on the Internet. This is a direct by-product of the freedom so highly cherished by Net citizens. When someone has an idea for doing something, he or she puts it out there and lets the Internet community decide its merits. As a result, it's difficult to put down in writing the *one exact* way to send email, search for information, or whatever.

There are also differences in the workings of a PC or Mac and the various versions of the two major Web browsers, Netscape and Microsoft Internet Explorer. If you can't find a particular command or function mentioned in the book, chances are it's there, but in a different place or with a slightly different name. Check the manual or online help that came with your computer, or ask a more computer-savvy friend or professor.

If learning about the Internet is making you a little nervous, relax! Getting up to speed takes a little time, but the effort will be well rewarded. Approach learning your way around the Internet with the same enthusiasm and curiosity you approach learning your way around a new college campus. This isn't a competition. Nobody's keeping score. And the only winner will be you.

Introducing the World Wide Web

If you've never seriously used the Web, you are about to take your first steps on what can only be described as an incredible journey. Just as no one owns the Internet, there is no formal organization among the collection of hundreds of thousands of computers that make up the part of the Net called the World Wide Web.

Initially, you might find it convenient to think of the Web as cable television with millions of channels. It's safe to say that, among all these channels, there's something for you to watch. Only, how do you find it? You could click through the channels one by one, of course, but by the time you found something of interest it would either (1) be over or (2) leave you wondering if there wasn't something better on that you're missing.

A more efficient way to search for what you want would be to consult some sort of TV listing. While you could skim through pages more rapidly than channels, the task would still be daunting. A more creative approach would allow you to press a button on your remote control that would connect you to a channel of interest; what's more, that channel would contain the names (or numbers) of other channels with similar programs. Those channels in turn would contain information about other channels. Now you could zip through this million-channel universe, touching down only at programs of potential interest.

If you have a feel for how this might work for television, you have a feel for what it's like to journey around (or "surf") the Web. Instead of channels, we have *Web sites*. Each site contains one or more *pages*. Each page may contain links to other pages, either in the same site or in other sites, anywhere in the world. These other pages may elaborate on the information you're looking at, direct you to related but not identical information, or even provide contrasting or contradictory points of view. And, of course, these pages could have links of their own.

Today, Web sites are maintained by businesses, institutions, affinity groups, professional organizations, government departments, and ordinary people anxious to express opinions, share information, sell products, or provide services. Because these sites are stored electronically, updating them is more convenient and practical than updating printed media. That makes Web sites far more dynamic than other types of research material you may be used to, and it means a visit to a Web site can open up new opportunities that weren't available as recently as a few hours ago.

part

1

Hypertext and Links

The invention that unveils these revolutionary possibilities is called *hypertext*. Hypertext is a technology for combining text, graphics, sounds, video, and links on a single World Wide Web page. Unlike traditional linear documents such as books, hypertext allows navigation through pages in any order that you like. Click on a link and you're transported, like Alice falling down the rabbit hole, to a new page, a new address, a new environment for research and communication.

Links come in three flavors: text, picture, and hot spot. A text link may be a letter, a word, a phrase, a sentence, or any contiguous combination of text characters. You can identify text links at a glance because the characters are <u>underlined</u> and often displayed in a unique color, setting the link apart from the rest of the text on the page. Picture links may be drawings, photos, or other graphic elements. On the Web, a picture may not only be worth a thousand words, but also the start of a journey into a whole new corner of cyberspace.

The hot spot is neither underlined nor bordered. It would be impossible to see were it not for a Web convention that offers you (literally) a helping hand for finding all types of links. Whenever the mouse cursor

part
1

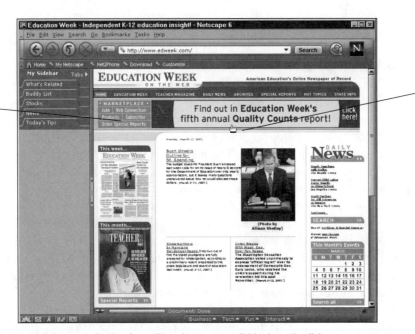

Text links are underlined and set off in color. You can tell this picture is a link because the mouse cursor has changed from an arrow to a hand.

passes over a link, the cursor changes from an arrow to a hand. Wherever you see the hand icon, you can click and retrieve another Web page. Sweep the cursor over an area of interest, see the hand, follow the link, and you're surfing the Web. Hot spots are sometimes located on areas of a large picture called an "image map." Clicking on different areas of the image map will lead you to different Web pages.

In the Name of the Page

Zipping around the Web in this way may seem exciting, even serendipitous, but it's also fraught with peril. How, for instance, do you revisit a page of particular interest? Or share a page with a classmate? Or cite a page as a reference for a professor? Web page designers assign titles to their pages; unfortunately, there's nothing to prevent two designers from assigning the same title to different pages.

An instrument that uniquely identifies Web pages does exist. It's called a *Universal Resource Locator (URL)*. A URL contains all the information necessary to locate the:

part

1

- ■ Web page containing the information you're looking for;
- ■ computer that hosts (stores) that page of information;
- ■ form in which the information is stored.

A typical URL looks like this:

```
http://www.abacon.com/index.html
```

You enter it into the **Location** or **Address** field at the top of your browser window. Hit the **Return** (or **Enter**) key, and your browser will deliver to your screen the exact page specified. When you click on a link, you're actually using a shorthand alternative to typing the URL yourself because the browser does it for you. In fact, if you watch the "Location" or "Address" field when you click on a link, you'll see its contents change to the URL to which you're traveling.

The URL Exposed

How does your browser know where you're going? As arcane as the URL appears, there is a logical explanation to its apparent madness. This is true not only of URLs, but also of computers in general. Because a computer's "intelligence" only extends to following simple instructions exactly, most of the commands, instructions, and procedures you'll encounter have simple underlying patterns. Once you familiarize yourself with these patterns, you'll find you're able to make major leaps in your understanding of new Internet features.

To unscramble the mysteries of Web addresses, we'll start at the end of the URL and work our way toward the front.

```
/index.html
```

This is the name of a single file or document. Eventually, the contents of this file/document will be transferred over the Internet to your computer. However, because there are undoubtedly thousands of files on the Internet with this name, we need to clarify our intentions a bit more.

```
www.abacon.com
```

This is the name of a particular Internet *Web server,* a computer whose job it is to forward Web pages to you on request. By Internet convention, this name is unique. The combination of

```
www.abacon.com/index.html
```

identifies a unique file/document on a unique Web server on the World Wide Web. No other file has this combined address, so there's no question about which file/document to transfer to you.

The characters *http://* at the beginning of the URL identify the method by which the file/document will be transferred. The letters stand for HyperText Transfer Protocol.

You Can Go Home (and to Other Pages) Again

You know that a URL uniquely identifies a Web page and that links let you travel from page to page, but what if you end up at a dead end? Missing page messages take several forms, such as "URL 404," "Object not on this server," "Missing Object," or "Page Not Found," but they all tell you that the page specified by the link or URL no longer exists.

There are many reasons for missing pages. You may have entered the URL incorrectly (every character must be precise and no spaces are allowed). More than likely, though, especially if you arrived here via a link, the page you're after has been moved or removed. Remember, anybody can create a link to any page. That's the good news. The bad news is that the owner of a page is under no obligation to inform the owners of links pointing to it that the page location has changed. In fact, there's no way for the page owner to even know about all the links to that page. Yes, the Internet's spirit of independence proves frustrating sometimes, but you'll

Don't Be Lost In (Hyper)Space

Let's pause for a quick check of your Web navigation skills. Look at the sample Web page below. How many links does it contain?

Did you find four? The four links include:

1. The word "links" in the second line below the seaside picture;

2. The sentence "What about me?";

3. The word "cyberspace" in the quick brown fox sentence;

4. The hot spot in the seaside picture. We know there's at least one link in the picture, because the cursor appears as a hand. (There may be more hot spots on the page, but we can't tell from this picture alone.)

A sample web page to exercise your link identifying skills.

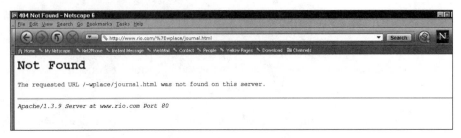

A missing page message, an all too common road hazard on the information superhighway.

find these small inconveniences are a cheap price to pay for the benefits you receive. Philosophy aside, though, we're still stuck on a page of no interest to us. The best strategy is to back up and try another approach.

Every time you click on the **Back** button (or back arrow in Netscape 6) at the top of the browser, you return to the previous page visited. That's because your browser keeps track of the pages you visit and the order in which you visit them. The **Back** button, and its counterpart, the **Forward** button (or forward arrow in Netscape 6), allow you to retrace the steps of your cyberpath.

What if you want to move two, three, or a dozen pages at once? Although you can click the **Back** or **Forward** buttons multiple times, Web browsers offer an easier navigation shortcut. If you use Netscape, clicking on the **Go** menu in the menu bar displays a list of your most recently visited pages, in the order in which you visited them. Unlike the **Back** or **Forward** buttons, you can select any page from the menu, and a single click takes you directly there. There's no need to laboriously move one page a time. If you use Internet Explorer, you can click on the **History** button in the Explorer bar or press the arrow at the end of the Address bar to see a list of links you visited in previous days and weeks.

Suppose you want to return to a page hours, days, or even months later. One way is to write down the URL of every page you may want to revisit. There's got to be a better way, and there is: We call them *bookmarks* (in Netscape) or *favorites* (in Microsoft Internet Explorer).

Like their print book namesakes, bookmarks (and favorites) flag specific Web pages. Selecting an item from the **Bookmark/Favorites** menu, like selecting an item from the **Go** menu, is the equivalent of entering a URL into the **Location** field of your browser, except that items in the **Bookmark/Favorites** menu are ones you've added yourself and represent pages visited over many surfing experiences, not just the most recent one.

In Netscape 6, to save a favorite Web page, pull down the **Bookmarks** menu and click on the **Add Current Page** command. When you want to select a page from your bookmark list, just click on the desired entry. To edit the title or URL of a bookmark, choose **Manage Bookmarks.** This feature also lets you arrange your favorites in folders by category.

Selecting **Add to Favorites** from the **Favorites** menu performs the same function as Bookmarks in Netscape 6 and adds the location of the current page to your list of favorite pages. If you want to be able to review this page when you're not online, click on the "Make available offline" checkbox.

A cautionary note is in order here. Your Bookmark or Favorites list physically exists only on your personal computer, which means that if you connect to the Internet on a different computer, your list won't be available. However, if you routinely connect to the Internet from a computer lab, there is a way to avoid the work of retyping your URLs each time you use a different computer. Both Internet Explorer and Netscape provide procedures to save favorites in a computer file that you can move from one computer to another. You can export a selected folder in your Favorites list, or all of your favorites. Since exported favorites are saved as an HTML file, either Internet Explorer or Navigator can import them.

In Internet Explorer 5.5, under the File menu, choose **Import and Export** to pull up the Import/Export Wizard. Follow the on-screen instructions to **Export Favorites.** You will see a list of files. Insert a blank diskette into the diskette drive and choose the diskette drive on which you want to export the favorites. When you begin working on a different computer, insert your diskette with the file of favorites into the diskette drive. Again choose Import and Export from the File menu and follow the on-screen instructions to **Import Favorites.** Click on Browse to indicate where you want to import the favorites.

In Netscape 6, click on **Bookmarks,** and then **Manage Bookmarks.** Then, in the window that opens, select **Export Bookmarks** from under the File menu. A list of files on your hard drive will appear. Insert a blank diskette and click on the arrow beside the "Save in" prompt to change the drive. When you begin working on a different computer, insert your diskette with the file of bookmarks into the diskette drive. Again, click on Bookmarks, Manage Bookmarks, and select **Import Bookmarks** from the File menu. Locate the filename of your bookmarks in the browser window and open it. Your bookmark file will now open when you choose Bookmarks.

part

1

Quick Check

As a quick review, here's what we know about navigating the Web so far:

- Enter a URL directly into the Location field;
- Click on a link;
- Use the **Back** or **Forward** icons;
- Select a page from the **Go** menu.
- Add bookmarks or favorite URLs.

Searching and Search Engines

Returning to our cable television analogy, you may recall that we glossed over the question of how we selected a starting channel in the first place. With a million TV channels, or several million Web pages, we can't depend solely on luck guiding us to something interesting.

On the Web, we solve the problem with specialized computer programs called *search engines* that crawl through the Web, page by page, cataloging its contents. As different software designers developed search strategies, entrepreneurs established Web sites where any user could find pages containing particular words and phrases. Today, Web sites such as Yahoo! offer you a "front door" to the Internet that begins with a search for content of interest.

The URLs for some popular search sites are:

AltaVista	www.altavista.com
Excite	www.excite.com
Google	www.google.com
HotBot	www.hotbot.lycos.com
Infoseek	www.infoseek.com
MetaCrawler	www.metacrawler.com

WebCrawler   `www.webcrawler.com`

Yahoo!   `www.yahoo.com`

Internet Gold Is Where You Find It

Let's perform a simple search using Hotbot to find information about the history of the Internet. See the results in the screen shown below and on pages 14–16.

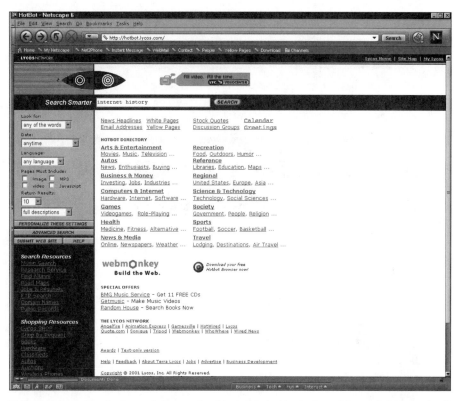

We'll start by searching for the words "internet" or "history." By looking for "any of the words," the search will return pages on which either "internet" or "history" or both appear.

Our search returned more than 50 million matches or *hits.* Pages are ranked according to the following factors: words in the title, keyword meta tags, word frequency in the document, and document length.

We can conduct the same search, but this time look for "all the words." The search will return hits when both "internet" and "history" appear on the same page, in any order, and not necessarily next to each other.

The search is narrowed down somewhat, but still has more than 5 million hits. You'll note that HotBot has provided a Top 10 list of results for this search.

When we search for the exact phrase "internet history," which means those two words in exactly that order, with no intervening words, we're down to several thousand hits (still a substantial number).

Now the first hits may be more specific. However, other hits in the list may have nothing to do with the history of the Internet. Hits happen. No search engine is 100 percent accurate 100 percent of the time. Spurious search results are the serendipity of the Internet. Look at them as an opportunity to explore something new.

Clearly, narrowing down your search as much as possible is essential. Click on Help in the Search area on the left side of the HotBot page to obtain tips for narrowing your search. You'll find search tip pages like this at all the major search engine sites.

Out of curiosity, let's try our history of the Internet search using a different search engine. When we search for the phrase "history of the internet" using WebCrawler, the quotation marks serve the same purpose as selecting "the exact phrase" option in HotBot. But the Web-Crawler search only finds approximately 900 hits. Some are the same as those found using HotBot, some are different. Different searching strategies and software algorithms make using more than one search engine a must for serious researchers.

The major search engines conveniently provide you with tips to help you get the most out of their searches. These include ways to use AND and OR to narrow down searches, and ways to use NOT to eliminate unwanted hits.

Each search engine also uses a slightly different approach to cataloging the Web, so your results may vary. Often, one search engine provides better results (more relevant hits) in your areas of interest; sometimes the wise strategy is to provide the same input to several different engines. No one search engine does a perfect job all the time, so experience will dictate the one that's most valuable to you.

part

1

Quick Check

Let's review our searching strategies:

- Visit one of the search engine sites;
- Enter key words or phrases that best describe the search criteria;
- Narrow the search if necessary by using options such as "all the words" or "the exact phrase." On some search engines, you may use the word "and" or the symbol "|" to indicate words that all must appear on a page;
- Try using the same criteria with different search engines.

Additional Internet Resources

Developed by the University of Minnesota, **Gopher** was an early method for navigating the Internet. Where did it get its name? Some say a gopher was the university's mascot, but the name also sounds like "go for." And what you go for are files at a Gopher site. The contents are listed in a hierarchical menu with folders containing files. Text files can be read in a window. Gopher sites are still run by some universities. You can use your Web browser to connect by typing gopher://*name of site* in the location box.

Telnet is a program used to access remote databases, library catalogs, and MUDs/MOOs (discussed later in this chapter). Telnet uses Unix commands and is not very user-friendly. Some universities have telnet sites that require you to have an account on their server. Other sites let you log in as a guest. You can access a telnet site with your Web browser by typing telnet://*address of site*. A menu of options will appear.

File Transfer Protocol (FTP) is a method for sending (*uploading*) and receiving (*downloading*) files over the Internet. These files may be free software, text, graphics, audio, or video. Anonymous FTP sites allow anyone to log in as "anonymous" and use an email address as a password. For a list of FTP sites and tutorials, see FTPplanet.com at www.ftpplanet.com.

To access an FTP site with your Web browser, just enter the address in the location box by typing ftp://*address of site*. Once you are connected, you will see a directory listing with folder icons and document files. Special FTP client programs make it easy to send and receive files, or to transfer more than one file at a time. They are often used for managing Web sites. An example is WS_FTP, which you can download at www.ipswitch.com/pd_wsftp.html.

Plug-Ins Bring the Web to Life

Plug-ins are free software that allow Web pages to include audio, video, or animation. Some plug-ins, such as RealPlayer (audio and video) and Netscape Radio (live radio), are now included with Netscape. Others must be downloaded and installed before they can be used. These files may be compressed and need a utility program such as WinZip for Windows (www.winzip.com) or Stuffit for the Mac (www.aladdinsys.com) to decompress them.

Here are five plug-ins and where to get more information:

- Macromedia ShockWave makes it possible to view complex animations and engage in interactions with the software. See www.macromedia.com/shockwave.
- RealAudio compresses audio files and transmits them over the Internet. It uses a technique called "streaming audio" so that the

sound will start to play while the file is still downloading. The RealAudio Player appears in a separate window on your monitor. See www.realaudio.com.

- QuickTime Video was developed by Apple Computer, Inc. The QuickTime Player lets you play video files. There are versions for both the PC and the Mac. See quicktime.apple.com.

- The Macromedia Flash Viewer enables you to view animated text or graphics. It is also used for animated slide shows, games, and educational interactions. See www.macromedia.com.

- The Adobe Acrobat Viewer lets you view and print files created in Adobe Portable Document Format, a way of storing pages with complex layout. See www.adobe.com/products/acrobat/readermain.html.

Give Your Web Browser Some Personality—Yours

Email and newsgroups let you communicate with others through the Internet at your own pace and on your own time. Before you can access these functions, however, you must set up or personalize your browser. If you always work on the same computer, this is a one-time operation in which you tell your browser where to find essential computer servers, along with personal information the Internet needs to move messages for you.

Begin by setting up your desired home page. This is the page that you will see whenever you first log on to the Internet. You can return to this page at any time by clicking on the **Home** icon. For example, for your convenience, you may want your browser to start by fetching your favorite search site or your school library's home page. Both Netscape 6 and Internet Explorer 5.5 offer the option of a blank home page. In that case, you will get a blank browser window.

To set up your home page in Netscape 6, go to the **Edit** menu and click on **Preferences.** Type in the URL of the page you want to use as your home page. The Appearance tab lets you set up Web preferences such as the color of links and visited links (the default is blue and purple), style and size of fonts, themes (look of buttons and toolbars) history (how long to keep a list of pages you've visited), the layout of mail and newsgroups messages, and advanced options. In Internet Explorer 5.5, you can set up a home page through the **Internet Options** found under the **Tools** menu.

part

1

Next, set up your browser for mail and newsgroup operation. You need to know the name of the mail and news servers along with your user name and other details, such as the address of the domain name server (DNS) of your ISP. You should have received all this information when you opened your Internet account. If not, ask for it. Help provided by the Windows and Mac operating systems will automatically enter some of this information for you.

Netscape 6 differs from earlier versions of this browser in that it makes it possible to set up several email accounts using different servers. Each account has a separate inbox for receiving mail. For each account, you create an account name and server settings such as server type, server name, user name, and port. An area for mail folders appears on the left, while an area for a list of the mail you've received will appear on the right, including the Subject, Sender, and Date.

To set up your email and newsgroup accounts with Netscape 6, under the **Tasks** menu, select **Mail.** Choose **Edit** and then **Mail/News Account Settings** to activate the Account Wizard. The Account Settings menu will appear. Enter the type of account you want to set up: email, WebMail (Netscape's own email service), America Online, or newsgroup. Enter your name and email address and click on Next. The information you are asked to enter next depends on the type of account you are setting up.

For example, if setting up an email account, be sure to use your user name (and not your alias) in the "Account Name" field. Your Reply To address is typically the same as your email address, though if you have an email alias you can use it here. You can attach a signature such as a favorite saying to each piece of mail you send. You can also choose to write your messages in plain text or in HTML.

Now highlight the **Server** category to tell the browser where to find your mail servers. The SMTP server handles your outgoing messages, while the POP3 or IMAP mail server routes incoming mail. The outgoing SMTP server is usually the same for all accounts, including newsgroups. Indicate how often you want Netscape to check for new messages (the default is every 10 minutes).

To add a new account, click the **New Account** button. Again, select the type of account. For example, if you choose newsgroup, you must enter the name of your news (NNTP) server such as "news.netscape.net" by highlighting the Server category. The Internet Connection Wizard may automatically enter the newsgroup server name your ISP has provided. Again, be sure to specify how often Netscape should check for new messages. If you do not do this, you will have to click on the Get Msg button to retrieve messages.

part

1

Click on OK in the bottom right part of the window when finished adding your accounts. This will save the information.

Netscape 6 also lets you choose the font style and color for email and newsgroup messages. Just go to **Edit, Preferences, Mail and Newsgroups,** and then click on **Message Display.** You can choose whether to wrap text or display emoticons (e.g., little smiley faces) as graphics. If you click on **Message Composition,** you can indicate whether you want a message to which you are replying to be quoted within your email and where it will appear. To set up automatic address collection, select **Address Books.**

In Internet Explorer 5.5, the Internet Connection Wizard will help you set up the email server and newsgroup (NNTP) server provided by your ISP. Go to the Tools menu and choose Internet Options. Then click on the Setup button to bring up the wizard. You can view or modify how your server connections are set up by clicking on **Internet Options** under the **Tools** menu. Click on the **Connections** tab and then **Settings and Properties.** Finally, click on **Server Types** for information about your dial-up server to the Internet.

To select an email program to use, from the **Internet Options** window click on **Programs.** A list of email services will come up to choose from, such as Hotmail, Microsoft Outlook, Outlook Express, or America Online. You can also indicate whether you want to use HTML to write your email messages. Then click on **Newsgroups** to select a newsgroup program.

part

1

The (E)mail Goes Through

Email was one of the first applications created for the Internet by its designers. Your electronic Internet mailbox is to email what a post office box is to "snail mail" (the name Net citizens apply to ordinary, hand-delivered mail). This mailbox resides on the computer of your ISP. The Internet doesn't deliver a message to your door but instead leaves it in a conveniently accessible place (your mailbox) in the post office (the computer of your ISP), until you retrieve the mail using your combination (password).

If you currently have access to the Internet, your school or ISP assigned you a *username* (also called a user id, account name, or account number). This username may be your first name, your first initial and the first few characters of your last name, or some strange combination of numbers and letters only a computer could love. An email address is a combination of your username and the unique address of the computer through which you access your email. For example:

```
username@computername.edu
```

The three letters after the dot, in this case "edu," identify the top level "domain." There are six common domain categories in use: edu (educational), com (commercial), org (organization), net (network), mil (military), and gov (government). The symbol "@"—called the "at" sign—serves two purposes: For computers, it provides a neat, clean separation between your username and the computer name; for people, it makes Internet addresses more pronounceable. Your address is read: username "at" computer name "dot" e-d-u. Suppose your Internet username is "a4736g" and your ISP is Allyn & Bacon, the publisher of this book. Your email address might look like

```
a4736g@abacon.com
```

and you would tell people your email address is "ay-four-seven-three-six-gee at ay bacon dot com."

We Don't Just Handle Your Email, We're Also a Client

You use email with the aid of special programs called *mail clients*. As with search engines, mail clients have the same set of core features, but your access to these features varies with the type of program. On both the PC and the Mac, Netscape and Microsoft Internet Explorer give you access to mail clients while you're plugged into the Web. That way you can pick up and send mail while you're surfing the Web. The basic email service functions are creating and sending mail, reading mail, replying to mail, and forwarding mail. First we'll examine the process of sending and reading mail, and then we'll discuss how to set up your programs so that your messages arrive safely.

Let's look at a typical mail client screen, in this case from Netscape 6. You reach this screen by choosing **Mail** from the **Tasks** menu. The **Mail Toolbar** appears across the top of the Netscape Mail window. Under the toolbar and to the left appear the folders contained in each email account, such as Inbox, Unsent Messages, Drafts, Sent, and Trash. The Message List window lists the current mail, including the Subject, Sender, and Date. The first message appears in a message window. Click on the Next button to read the next new message. You can choose how to sort messages by choosing **Sort** from the **View** menu.

```
┌──────────────────────────────────────────────────────────────┐
│ N Create Mail - Netscape 6                                  ⊠ │
│ ┌──────────────────────────────────────────────────────────┐ │
│ │ N Netscape      Write a Message              WebMail Help │ │
│ ├──────────────────────────────────────────────────────────┤ │
│ │   ⊡       ⊟       ⊞        ⊗                               │ │
│ │  Send  Add Addresses  Save As Draft  Cancel               │ │
│ │                                                           │ │
│ │    To: [                                              ]   │ │
│ │    Cc: [                                              ]   │ │
│ │   Bcc: [                                              ]   │ │
│ │ Subject: [                                            ]   │ │
│ │                                                           │ │
│ │ Type Your Message Here:                                   │ │
│ │ ┌──────────────────────────────────────────────────────┐ │ │
│ │ │                                                      │ │ │
│ │ │                                                      │ │ │
│ │ │                                                      │ │ │
│ │ │                                                      │ │ │
│ │ └──────────────────────────────────────────────────────┘ │ │
│ │ Attachments:  ┌──────────┐ ▲ [ Add...  ]                  │ │
│ │               │          │ ▼ [ Delete  ]                  │ │
│ │               └──────────┘                                │ │
│ │  Send  Add Addresses  Save As Draft  Cancel               │ │
│ │ © 2000 Netscape, All rights reserved. Legal & Privacy Notices.  WebMail Help │ │
│ └──────────────────────────────────────────────────────────┘ │
└──────────────────────────────────────────────────────────────┘
```

New message form, with fields for recipient's address and the subject, and a window for the text of the message.

To send an email message, from the **File** menu choose **New,** then **Message.** If the mail window is already open, an easier method is to click on the **New Msg** button from the Mail toolbar. This creates a blank Message Compose window that has a "from" field for your address, a "to" field for the recipient's address, a subject field, and a window in which to type the text of the message. Type the address or select a recipient from the automated Address Book by clicking on the **Address** button. You can attach a file to your message with the **Attach** button. To save a copy of your message, click on **Save.**

Fill in the recipient's address in the "To" field, just above the arrow. Use your own address. We'll send email to ourselves and use the same message to practice sending email and reading it as well; then you'll know if your messages come out as expected. Click in the "Subject" field and enter a word or phrase that generally describes the topic of the message. Since we're doing this for the first time, let's type "Maiden Email Voyage." Click anywhere in the text window and enter your message: "Hi. Thanks for guiding me through sending my first email." You'll find that the mail client works here like a word processing program, which means you can insert and delete words and characters and highlight text.

When you've finished the message, click on the **Send** button. You've just created and sent your first email message. In most systems, it takes from a few seconds to a few minutes for a message to yourself to reach your mailbox, so you might want to take a short break before continuing. When you're ready to proceed, close the Compose window and click the **Get Msg** button on the Mail window toolbar to receive your message. The first time you retrieve a message from an email account, you will be asked to enter a password.

In Internet Explorer 5.5, the appearance of the mail client screen will depend on your email program. Pull up the **Tools** menu and select **Mail and News.** This menu lets you read mail or send a new message. For example, to use the Microsoft Express email program, select **New Message** and click on OK to open a message window. Type your message and click on **Send.** Click on **Tools** and then **Address Book** to set up a list of contacts.

part
1

What Goes Around Comes Around

Now let's retrieve the message you just sent to yourself. When retrieving mail, most mail clients display a window showing the messages in your mailbox and telling you how many new messages have been added.

If you've never used your email before, chances are that your message window is empty, or contains only one or two messages (usually official messages from the ISP) besides the one you sent to yourself. The message to yourself should be accompanied by an indicator of some sort—such as a closed envelope icon—indicating it's a new message. You also get to see the date of the message, who sent it, and the information you entered in the subject line. The Subject field lets you scan your messages and determine which ones you want to look at first.

The summary of received messages tells you everything you need to know about a message except what's in it. Click anywhere on the line to see the contents in the message window. Click on the message from yourself and you'll see the contents of the message displayed in a window. The information at the top—To, From, Subject, and so forth—is called the *header.* Depending on your system, you may also see some cryptic lines with terms such as X-Mailer, received by, and id number. Most of the time, there's nothing of interest in this part of the header, so just skip over it for now.

Moving Forward

The contents, or text, of your message can be cut and pasted just like any other text document. If you and a classmate are working on a project together, your partner can write part of a paper and email it to you, and you can copy the text from your email message and paste it into your word processing program.

What if there are three partners in this project? One partner sends you a draft of the paper for you to review. You like it and want to send it on to your other partner. The **Forward** feature lets you send the message intact, so you don't have to cut and paste it into a new message window.

To forward a message, highlight it in the Inbox (top) and click the Forward icon. Enter the recipient's address in the "To" field of the message window. Note that the subject of the message is "Fwd:" followed by the subject of the original message. Use the text window to add your comments ahead of the original message.

A Chance to Reply

Email is not a one-way message system. Let's reply to the message you sent yourself by clicking on the **Reply** icon. What you see next depends on how you set up your Netscape 6 Preferences for Mail and Newsgroups, Message Composition. You were given the choice of quoting the original message within the text of your reply ("inline") or including the original message as an attachment. If you chose inline, you could also indicate if you wanted the quoted message to appear above or below any new text that you added for your reply. Let's assume that you chose "inline" and to have the quoted message appear above your new message.

Depending on which email program you're using, you'll see that each line in the quoted message is preceded by either a vertical bar or a right angle bracket. Note that the "From" and "To" fields have been filled in automatically and that the "Subject" field contains the original subject preceded by "Re." The vertical bar or > is used to indicate lines written by someone else (in this case, the message's original author). Why bother? Because this feature allows you to reply without retyping the parts of the message to which you're responding. Because your typing isn't quoted, your answers stand out from the original message.

part

1

A Discussion of Lists

There's no reason you can't use email to create a discussion group. You pose a question, for example, by sending an email message to everyone in the group. Somebody answers and sends the answer to everyone else on the list, and so on. At least that's the theory.

In practice, this is what often happens. As people join and leave the group, you and the rest of your group are consumed with updating your lists, adding new names and deleting old ones. As new people join, their addresses may not make it onto the lists of all the members of the group, so different participants get different messages. The work of administering the lists becomes worse than any value anyone can get out of the group, and so it quickly dissolves.

Generally, you're better off letting the computer handle discussion group administration. A *listserv* or *electronic mailing list* is a program for administering email to lists of subscribers. It automatically adds and deletes list members and handles the distribution of messages.

Thousands of mailing lists have already been formed by users with common interests. You may find mailing lists for celebrities, organizations, political interests, occupations, and hobbies. Your instructor may establish a mailing list for your course. For a list of searchable listservs, see www.liszt.com. Listservs come in several different flavors. Some are extremely active. You can receive as many as forty or more email messages a day. Other lists may send you a message a month. One-way lists, such as printed newsletters, do not distribute your reply to any other subscriber. Some lists distribute replies to everyone. These lists include mediated lists, in which an "editor" reviews each reply for suitability (relevance, tone, use of language) before distributing the message, and unmediated lists, in which each subscriber's response is automatically distributed to all the other subscribers with no restrictions except those dictated by decency and common sense, though these qualities may not always be obvious from reading the messages.

Get on a List Online

You join in the discussion by subscribing to a listserv, which is as straightforward as sending email. You need to know only two items: the name of the list and the address of the listserv program handling subscriptions.

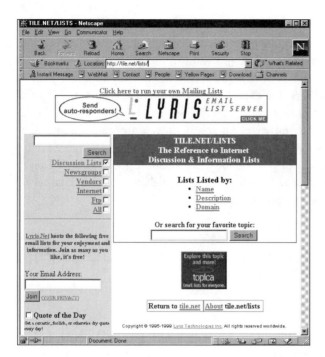

Tile.Net offers shortcuts to working your way through the Internet's maze of discussion lists.

To join a list, send a **Subscribe** message to the listserv administrative address (not necessarily the same as the listserv address, as the administrative address may serve a number of different lists). The message is usually as simple as "subscribe," the name of the list, and your name (your real name, not your username), all on one line. *And that's all.* This message will be read by a computer program that looks for these items only. At the very best, other comments in the message will be ignored; at the very worst, your entire message will be ignored. Within a few hours to a day after subscribing, the listserv will automatically send you a confirmation email message, including instructions for sending messages, finding out information about the list and its members, and canceling your subscription. Save this message for future reference. That way, if you do decide to leave the list, you won't have to circulate a message to the members asking how to unsubscribe, and you won't have to wade through fifty replies all relaying the same information you received when you joined.

Soon after your confirmation message appears in your mailbox, and depending on the activity level of the list, you'll begin receiving email messages. When you reply to a message, reply to the listserv address, not the address of the sender (unless you want your communication to remain private). The listserv program takes care of distributing your message listwide. Use the address in the "Reply To" field of the message. Most mail clients automatically use this address when you select the **Reply** command. Some may ask if you want to use the reply address (say yes). Some lists will send a copy of your reply to you so you know your message is online. Others don't send the author a copy, relying on your faith in the infallibility of computers.

You can cancel your subscription at any time. Simply send a message to the address you used to subscribe (which you'll find on that confirmation message you saved for reference), with "unsubscribe," followed on the same line by the name of the list. For example, to leave a list named "WRITER-L," you would send:

```
unsubscribe WRITER-L
```

Even if you receive messages for a short while afterwards, be patient—they will disappear.

Waste Not, Want Not

Listservs create an excellent forum for people with common interests to share their views; however, from the Internet standpoint, these lists are terribly wasteful. First of all, if there are a thousand subscribers to a list, every message must be copied a thousand times and distributed over the Internet. If there are forty replies a day, this one list creates forty thousand email messages. Ten such lists mean almost a half million messages, most of which are identical, flying around the Net.

Another wasteful aspect of listservs is the way in which messages are answered. The messages in your mailbox on any given day represent a combination of new topics and responses to previous messages. But where are these previous messages? If you saved them, they're in your email mailbox taking up disk space. If you haven't saved them, you have nothing to which to compare the response. What if a particular message touches off a chain of responses, with subscribers referring not only to the source message but to responses as well? It sounds like the only safe strategy is to save every message from the list, a suggestion as absurd as it is impractical.

What we really need is something closer to a bulletin board than a mailing list. On a bulletin board, messages are posted once. Similar notices wind up clustered together. Everyone comes to the same place to read or post messages.

And Now the News(group)

The Internet equivalent of the bulletin board is the Usenet newsgroup. Begun in 1979, today Usenet is a worldwide network of approximately 4,000 newsgroups. Usenet messages are copied only once for each ISP supporting the newsgroup. If there are a thousand students on your campus reading the same newsgroup message, there need only be one copy of the message stored on your school's computer.

Newsgroups are categorized by topics, with topics broken down nto subtopics and sub-subtopics. For example, you'll find newsgroups devoted to computers, hobbies, science, social issues, and "alternatives." Newsgroups in this last category cover a wide range of topics that may not appeal to the mainstream. Also in this category are beginning newsgroups.

Usenet names are amalgams of their topics and subtopics, separated by dots. If you were interested in a newsgroup dealing with, say, music, you might start with rec.music and move down to rec.music.radiohead, or rec.music.techno, and so forth. The naming scheme allows you to zero in on a topic of interest.

part

1

Getting into the News(group) Business

Most of the work of reading, responding to, and posting messages is handled by a news reader client program, accessible through both Netscape and Microsoft Internet Explorer. You can not only surf the Web and handle your mail via your browser, but also drop into your favorite newsgroups virtually all in one operation. For a list of newsgroups that can be searched by topic, see **http://www.liszt.com/news/**.

To reach newsgroups via Netscape 6, choose **Tasks** and then **Mail** to bring up the Mail window. Click on **File** and choose **Subscribe.** You will see a list of newsgroup categories and newsgroups. Click on the **Subscribe** column next to a newsgroup. A check mark will appear next to each newsgroup to which you subscribe. (Click **Unsubscribe** if you change your mind.) Now, click OK, and the subscribed newsgroups will be displayed in the Mail window. Double click on the one of current interest, and a list of messages posted will be displayed. For each message, you will see the subject, sender, and date. Click on a message to open its contents in a window.

The top part of this figure shows a listing of posted messages. While not visible from this black and white reproduction, a red indicator in the Subject column marks unread messages. Double-clicking on a message opens its contents into a window shown in the bottom part of this figure. You can reply to this message via the Reply icon, or get the next message using the Next icon.

part
1

To reply to a message, highlight the message you want to answer and click the **Reply** button, then **Send.** To post a message on a new topic, select a newsgroup, click the **New Msg** button, write your message, and click on the Send button. Click on the **Get Msg** button to see your message within the newsgroup listing.

To reach newsgroups with Internet Explorer 5.5, pull up the **Tools** menu and select **Mail and News.** Choose **Add Newsgroups** to pull up a list from which you can choose to subscribe. Click on the desired newsgroup to see a list of messages posted.

Often, messages contain "Re:" in their subject lines, indicating a response to a previous message (the letters stand for "Regarding"). Many news readers maintain *threads* for you. Threads are chains of messages and all responses to that message. These readers give you the option to read messages chronologically or to read a message followed by its responses.

When you subscribe to a newsgroup, your news reader will also keep track of the messages you've read so that it can present you with the newest (unread) ones. While older messages are still available to you, this feature guarantees that you stay up-to-date without any record keeping on your part. Subscribing to a newsgroup is free, and the subscription information resides on your computer. Newsgroups have no way of knowing who their subscribers are, and the same caveat that applies to bookmarks applies to newsgroups. Information about your subscriptions resides physically on the personal computer you're using. If you switch computers, as in a lab, your subscription information and history of read messages are beyond your reach.

Welcome to the Internet, Miss Manners

part

1

While we're on the subject of Internet communication, here are some *netiquette* (net etiquette) tips.

Email Tips. When you send email to someone, even someone who knows you well, all they have to look at are your words—there's no body language attached. That means there's no smile, no twinkle in the eye, no raised eyebrow; and especially, there's no tone of voice. What you write is open to interpretation. You may understand the context of a remark, but will your reader?

If you have any doubts about how your message will be interpreted, you might want to tack an *emoticon* onto your message. An emoticon is a face created out of keyboard characters. For example, there's the happy Smiley :-) (you have to look at it sideways . . . the parenthesis is its mouth), the frowning Smiley :-((Frownie?), the winking Smiley ;-), and so forth. Smileys are the body language of the Internet. Use them to put remarks into context. "Great" in response to a friend's suggestion means you like the idea. "Great :-(" changes the meaning to one of disappointment or sarcasm. (Want a complete list of emoticons? Try using "emoticon" as a keyword for a Web search.)

Keep email messages on target. One of the benefits of email is its speed. Reading through lengthy messages leaves the reader wondering when you'll get to the point. Use short subject headings to indicate what the message is about.

Email's speed carries with it a certain responsibility. Its ease of use encourages quick responses, but quick doesn't necessarily mean thoughtful. Once you hit the **Send** icon, that message is gone. There's no recall button. Think before you write, lest you feel the wrath of the modern-day version of your parents' adage: Answer in haste, repent at leisure.

Listserv Tips. New listserv subscribers customarily wait a while before joining the discussion. After all, you're electronically strolling into a room full of strangers; it's only fair to see what topics are being discussed before wading in with your own opinions. Otherwise, you're like the bore at the party who elbows his way into a conversation with "But enough about you, let's talk about me." You'll also want to avoid the faux pas of posting a long missive on a topic that subscribers spent the preceding three weeks thrashing out.

Observe the list for a while. Understand its tone and feel, what topics are of interest to others and what areas are taboo. Also, look for personalities. Who's the most vociferous? Who writes very little but responds thoughtfully? Who's the most flexible? The most rigid?

Most of all, keep in mind that there are far more observers than participants. What you write may be read by 10 or 100 times more people than those whose names show up in the daily messages. Do not clutter up the list with "me, too" messages, or quote entire previous messages (only the part to which you're referring). Remember that messages arrive in the email box of subscribers and can fill it up.

Newsgroup Tips. Hang out for a while, or *lurk,* to familiarize yourself with the style, tone, and content of newsgroup messages. As you probably surmised from the names of the groups, their topics of discussion are quite narrow. One of the no-no's of newsgroups is posting messages on subjects outside the focus of the group. Posting off-topic messages, especially lengthy ones, is an excellent way to attract flaming.

A *flame* is a brutally debasing message from one user to another. Flames are designed to hurt and offend, and often the target of the flame feels compelled to respond in kind to protect his or her self-esteem. This leads to a *flame war,* as other users take sides and set flames of their own. If you find yourself the target of a flame, your best strategy is to ignore it. As with a campfire, if no one tends to the flames, they soon die out.

Keep your messages short and to the point. Many newsgroup visitors connect to the Internet via modems. Downloading a day's worth of long postings, especially uninteresting ones, is annoying and frustrating.

part

1

Similarly, don't post the same message to multiple, related newsgroups. This is called *cross posting,* and it's a peeve of Net citizens who check into these groups. If you've ever flipped the television from channel to channel during a commercial break only to encounter the same commercial (an advertising practice called *roadblocking*), you can imagine how annoying it is to drop in on several newsgroups only to find the same messages posted to each one.

With the huge potential audience newsgroups offer, you might think you've found an excellent medium for advertising goods or services. After all, posting a few messages appears analogous to running classified ads in newspapers, only here the cost is free. There's a name for these kinds of messages—*spam.* Spam is the junk mail of the Internet, and the practice of spamming is a surefire way to attract flames. The best advice for handling spam? Don't answer it. Not only does an answer encourage the spammer, but he or she will also undoubtedly put your email address on a list and sell it to other spammers, who will flood your online mailbox with their junk.

Above all, be considerate of others. Treat them the way you'd like to be treated. Do you enjoy having your grammar or word choices corrected in front of the whole world? Do you feel comfortable when someone calls you stupid in public? Do you appreciate having your religion, ethnicity, heritage, or gender belittled in front of an audience? Respect the rights and feelings of others, if not out of simple decency, then out of the sanctions your ISP may impose. Although you have every right to express an unpopular opinion or to take issue with the postings of others, most ISPs have regulations about the kinds of messages one can send via their facilities. Obscenities, threats, and spam may, at a minimum, result in your losing Internet access privileges.

part

1

Let's Chat

Virtual chatrooms let you communicate with others around the world in real time by typing on your keyboard. Unless moderated, chats tend to be rather chaotic, with comments going by fast and more than one conversation taking place at the same time!

When arriving in a chatroom, it's customary to say "hi" to whomever's there. Once you type a message, press Enter to send it. Since there may be a lag time between what you say and the answer, wait a few minutes. Do not type in all caps; this is SHOUTING. Describe your actions to make communication clearer (e.g., pounds on table for emphasis).

Types of chat programs include:

- *Web-based chat programs.* Web sites sometimes include a chatroom on a specific subject. Excite, AltaVista, and Yahoo all have free chatrooms. Look for a list of scheduled chats and topics.
- *Internet Relay Chat (IRC).* This method requires using special commands. An IRC server has chatrooms called "channels" where people talk, using nicknames. To use IRC, you need special software such as mIRC, a free program for the PC. You can download this program plus get instructions at the mIRC Homepage (www.geocities.com/~mirc).
- *ICQ.* ICQ ("I Seek You") began in 1997. ICQ networks contain lists of chatrooms. ICQ also lets you know when friends log on so that you can chat with them while still surfing the Internet. For this to work, both you and your friends must be using ICQ. See the official ICQ site at web.icq.com.

part

1

Netscape Instant Messenger is similar to chat in that communication occurs in real time. It is different in that messages are private, sent to an individual on a Buddy List that you create.

Virtual worlds, with either a social or educational function, also allow real-time chat. A *MUD (Multi-User Dimension)* or *MOO (Multi-user Object Oriented)* is a type of text-based virtual reality. It contains a narrative description of places, buildings, rooms, objects within rooms, and characters. You use special commands to chat with others, interact with objects, or create your own rooms and objects (with permission). Most MOOs or MUDs must be accessed through Telnet or a client program such as Tiny Fugue (tf.tcp.com/~hawkeye/tf/). Diversity University, an educational MOO, provides access through a Web Gateway located at http://moo.dumain.du.org:8000/, which makes it possible to see pictures.

Avatar virtual worlds contain two- or three-dimensional visual representations of a place. You choose a visual character called an "avatar" to represent yourself. You can chat with others or explore the world with special keys on your keyboard that allow you to walk, run, or fly! You must download special software to enter a virtual world. One example is ActiveWorlds at www.activeworlds.com. Try their free software, login as a visitor, and choose a world from the menu to visit.

Quick Check

Let's review the types of communication on the Internet:

- Email lets you send and receive letters electronically.
- A listserv lets you send email to a group of subscribers, and receive messages from anyone in that group.
- A newsgroup is like a bulletin board on which messages can be written and responded to by anyone at any time.
- Chat occurs in real time in a virtual chatroom.
- MUDs and MOOs are virtual text-based worlds. Avatar worlds have graphical representations of places and characters.

A Site of One's Own

part

1

Nowadays it's getting easier and easier for the average person to create his or her own Web pages. The advantages of having your own Web site are numerous: you can publish your papers and reports, post your resume, and even create photo albums of your family and friends. You need only three things to create a Web page: a file written in HTML (HyperText Markup Language), a server (a computer program that moves information on request) on which you can store your files, and a file transfer protocol (FTP) program to get your files onto the server.

Writing in HTML is very easy, and there are many resources on the Web that you can check out to learn the fundamentals. A good place to begin is *A Beginner's Guide to HTML* from the National Center for Supercomputing Applications (NCSA) at **http://www.ncsa.uiuc.edu/ General/Internet/WWW/HTMLPrimer.html** and a *Web Authoring Reference* from the Web Design Group at **http://www.htmlhelp.com.**

But, you don't even have to know HTML to create Web pages. If you use the tools in Netscape or software such as Microsoft's FrontPage or Macromedia's Dreamweaver, you can design Web pages without learning any HTML at all (though knowing a bit about HTML really comes in handy!). With Netscape 6 choose **Tasks** and then **Composer** to use Netscape Composer, easy-to-use page creation software. If you have

Internet Explorer 5.5, choose **File**, then **Edit with MS FrontPage** to work on your web site.

Access to space on a server is offered by many colleges and universities as well as a number of commercial organizations. Internet Service Providers such as Earthlink and AOL also offer space on their servers for a fee. Companies such as Yahoo! (**http://geocities.yahoo.com/home/**) and Tripod (**http://www.tripod.lycos.com**) provide free server space as well as page builder software. You may have to put up with some advertisements thrown onto your site, but if you can't afford to buy server space, this is a good option. Remember: only when your files reside on a server can your Web pages be accessed through the Internet.

FTP client programs will help you transfer the HTML files you create on your personal computer to the server. You can download one of these programs, WS_FTP, at **http://www.ipswitch.com/pc_wsftp.html**. An evaluation copy is free for you to try for 30 days.

For more information on Web page creation, check out these sites:

- Introduction to HTML from Case Western Reserve University: **http://www.cwru.edu/help/introHTML/**
- HotWired, The Web Developer's Resource, from Webmonkey: **http://hotwired.lycos.com/webmonkey/**
- HTML Goodies by Dr. Joe Burns: **http://htmlgoodies.earthweb.com/**

Security Issues

How Not to Come Down with a Virus

Downloading files from the Internet allows less responsible Net citizens to unleash onto your computer viruses, worms, and Trojan horses, all dangerous programs that fool you into thinking they're doing one thing while they're actually erasing your hard disk or performing some other undesirable task. Protection is your responsibility.

One way to reduce the risk of contracting a virus is to download software from reliable sites. Corporations such as Microsoft and Apple take care to make sure downloadable software is virus free. So do most institutions that provide software downloads as a public service (such as the Stanford University archives of Macintosh software). Be especially careful with programs you find on someone's home page. If you're not sure about safe download sources, ask around in a newsgroup, talk to friends, or check with the information technology center on campus.

In addition, be careful about downloading suspicious-looking email attachments, especially from someone you don't know. Even if you know the person the message appears to be from, someone could have obtained their email address and used it to send you a virus. If the subject heading sounds strange, it's better to ask questions now than to download and be sorry later!

To protect your files, it's a good idea to buy and use a reliable virus program. Both Symantec and McAfee sell first-rate programs. Go to **http://www.symantec.com** to purchase Norton Antivirus software for either the PC or Mac. At **http://www.mcafee.com** you can get McAfee VirusScan for the PC or Dr. Solomon's Virex for the Mac. You can update these programs right from the Internet so they'll detect the most current viruses. Most of the time, these programs can disinfect files/ documents on your hard drive that contain viruses. Don't forget to check files on your diskettes as well.

Crude as it may sound, downloading programs from the Internet without using a virus check is like having unprotected sex with a stranger. While downloading software may not be life-threatening, imagine the consequences if your entire hard disk, including all your course work and software, is totally obliterated. It won't leave you feeling very good.

part

1

Keeping Things to Yourself

The Internet is not private. Information you pass around the Internet is stored on, or passed along by, computers that are accessible to others. Your ISP may provide member directories that list all subscribers and their addresses. Your activities at a Web site can be tracked, including which pages you visited. Cookies, files left on your hard drive by certain sites, make it easy for advertisers to find out your interests.

Just as you take care to protect your wallet or purse while walking down a crowded street, it's also a good practice to exercise caution with information you'd like to keep (relatively) private. Although computer system administrators take great care to ensure the security of this information, no scheme is completely infallible. Here are some security tips:

■ Exercise care when sending sensitive information such as credit card numbers, social security numbers, passwords, even telephone numbers and addresses in email. Your email message may pass through four or five computers en route to its destination, and at any of

these points, it can be intercepted and read by someone other than
the recipient.

■ Send personal information over the Web only if the page is secure.
Web browsers automatically encrypt information on secure pages,
and the information can only be unscrambled at the Web site that
created the secure page.

In Netscape 6.0, an "s" is added to "http" to indicate a secure
Web page. This indicates that a security system called SSL (Secure
Sockets Layer) is in place. (The earlier Netscape 4 showed a closed
padlock symbol.) From the menu, select **Tasks, Privacy and Security,**
to bring up the Netscape Security Manager. Click on the **Information**
tab to learn more about the security setting for the page (if available). Click on the **Applications** tab if you want Netscape to display
a warning before leaving secure sites or sending unencrypted
information.

In Internet Explorer 5.5, an icon of a closed lock displayed on
the bottom right of the browser indicates a secure site. When you
are sending information, you may receive a warning message if the
site is not secure. IE classifies Web pages as Trusted Sites, Restricted
Sites, or Internet (all other sites). To change the default security levels,
choose **Internet Options** from the **Tools** menu and then **Security.** For
each classification type, choose the **Default** level for a visual view
of the security setting (high, medium, or low). For example, Trusted
Sites are listed as low security. Move the slider to change the
level. For more detailed security information, choose the **Custom**
level.Remember that any files you store on your ISP's computer are
accessible to unscrupulous hackers. See if your ISP has a privacy
policy, and find out what it says. Consider whether you really want
to post a "member profile" with information about yourself.

■ Protect your password. Many Web client programs, such as mail
clients, maintain your password for you. That means anyone with
physical access to your computer can read your email. With a few
simple tools, someone can even steal your password. Never leave
your password on a lab computer. (Make sure the **Remember Password** or **Save Password** box is unchecked in any application that asks
for your password.) It helps to change your password often and use a
combination of letters and numbers meaningful only to you.

■ If shopping online, check for contact information such as a phone
number. Ask others about the vendor's reputation. Do not click on
links in email sent by advertisers (they're probably checking to see
if your email address is active). Consider getting a separate email

account from a free provider such as Excite or Onebox.com and using it for shopping.

- The contents of any message you post become public information, but in a newsgroup your email address also becomes public knowledge. Use common sense about posting information you or someone else expects to remain private. Many newsgroup postings are archived (stored for a long period of time) and can be searched by search engines.

Finally, remember that the Web in particular and the Internet in general are communications media with a far-reaching audience, and placing information on the Internet is tantamount to publishing it. Information can and will be read by people with different tastes and sensitivities. The Web tends to be self-censoring, so be prepared to handle feedback, both good and bad.

Using the Internet for Research: Critical Evaluation

part

1

Much of your time online will be spent on researching your chosen field. Typical research resources, such as journal articles, books, and other scholarly works, are reviewed by a panel of experts before being published. At the very least, any reputable publisher takes care to assure that the author is who he or she claims to be and that the work being published represents an informed point of view. When anyone can post anything in a Web site or to a newsgroup, the burden of assessing the relevance and accuracy of what you read falls to you. Rumors quickly grow into facts on the Internet simply because stories spread so rapidly that the "news" seems to be everywhere. Because the Internet leaves few tracks, in no time it's impossible to tell whether you are reading independent stories or the same story that's been around the world two or three times. Gathering information on the Internet may be quick, but verifying the quality of information requires a serious commitment.

Approach researching via the Internet with confidence, however, not trepidation. You'll find it an excellent workout for your critical evaluation skills. No matter what career you pursue, employers value an employee who can think critically and independently. Critical thinking is also the basis of problem solving, another ability highly valued. So, as you research your academic projects, be assured that you're simultaneously developing lifelong expertise.

The first tip for successful researching on the Internet is to always consider your source. A Web site's URL often alerts you to the sponsor of the site. Or, if your search takes you to a specific article within a site, go to the home page of the site and read about the sponsoring institution. CNN or MSNBC are established news organizations, and you can give the information you find at their sites the same weight you would give to their cablecasts. Likewise, major newspapers operate Web sites with articles reprinted from their daily editions or expanded stories written expressly for the Internet. On the other hand, if you're unfamiliar with the source or suspect its accuracy, treat the information the way you would any new data. Look for specifics—"66 percent of all voters" as opposed to "most voters"—and for information that can be verified, such as a cited report in another medium or information accessible through a Web site hosted by a credible sponsor.

Look for independent paths to the same information. This can involve careful use of search engines or visits to newsgroups with both similar and opposing viewpoints. Make sure that the "independent" information you find is truly independent. In newsgroups, don't discount the possibility of multiple postings, or that a posting in one group is nothing more than a quotation from a posting in another. Ways to verify independent paths include following sources (if any) back to their origins, contacting the person who posted a message and asking for clarification, or checking other media for verification.

In many cases, you can use your common sense to raise your comfort level about the soundness of the information. With both listservs and newsgroups, it's possible to lurk for a while to develop a feeling for the authors of various postings. Who seems the most authoritarian, and who seems to be "speaking" from emotion or bias? Who seems to know what he or she is talking about on a regular basis? Do these people cite their sources of information (a job or affiliation perhaps)? Do they have a history of thoughtful, insightful postings, or do their postings typically contain generalities, unjustifiable claims, or flames? On Web sites, where the information feels more anonymous, there are also clues you can use to test for authenticity. Verify who's hosting the Web site. If the host or domain name is unfamiliar to you, perhaps a search engine can help you locate more information. Measure the tone and style of the writing at the site. Does it seem consistent with the education level and knowledge base necessary to write intelligently about the subject?

When offering an unorthodox point of view, good authors supply facts, figures, and quotes to buttress their positions, expecting readers to be skeptical of their claims. Knowledgeable authors on the Internet follow these same commonsense guidelines. Be suspicious of authors who expect you to agree with their points of view simply because they've published them on the Internet. In one-on-one encounters, you frequently judge the authority and knowledge of the speaker using criteria you'd be hard-pressed to explain. Use your sense of intuition on the Internet, too.

As a researcher (and as a human being), the job of critical thinking requires a combination of healthy skepticism and rabid curiosity. Newsgroups and Web sites tend to focus narrowly on single issues (newsgroups more so than Web sites). Don't expect to find a torrent of opposing views on newsgroup postings; their very nature and reason for existence dampens free-ranging discussions. A newsgroup on *The X-Files* might argue about whether extraterrestrials exist, but not about whether the program is the premier television show on the air today. Such a discussion would run counter to the purposes of the newsgroup. Anyone posting such a message would be flamed, embarrassed, ignored, or otherwise driven away.

It's Okay to Be Critical

part

1

Your research responsibilities include searching for opposing views by visiting a variety of newsgroups and Web sites. It helps here to fall back on the familiar questions of journalism: who, what, when, where, and why.

Who else might speak knowledgeably on this subject? Enter that person's name into a search engine. You might be surprised to find whose work is represented on the Web. (For fun, one of the authors entered the name of a rock-and-roll New York radio disk jockey into MetaCrawler and was amazed to find several pages devoted to the DJ, including sound clips of broadcasts dating back to the 1960s, along with a history of his theme song.)

What event might shed more information on your topic? Is there a group or organization that represents your topic? Do they hold an annual conference? Are synopses of presentations posted on the sponsoring organization's Web site?

When do events happen? Annual meetings or seasonal occurrences can help you isolate newsgroup postings of interest.

Where might you find this information? If you're searching for information on wines, for example, check to see if major wine-producing regions, such as the Napa Valley in California or the

Rhine Valley in Germany, sponsor Web sites. These may point you to organizations or information not found in other searches. Remember, Web search engines are fallible; they don't find every site you need.

Why is the information you're searching for important? The answer to this question can lead you to related fields. New drugs, for example, are important not only to victims of diseases but to drug companies and the Food and Drug Administration as well.

Approach assertions from a skeptic's point of view. See if they stand up to critical evaluation or if you're merely emotionally attached to them. Imagine "What if . . . ?" or "What about . . . ?" scenarios that may disprove or at least call into question what you're reading. Try following each assertion you pull from the Internet with the phrase "on the other hand. . . ." Because you can't leave the sentence hanging, you'll be forced to finish it, and this will help get you into the habit of critically examining information.

These are, of course, the same techniques critical thinkers have employed for centuries, only now you are equipped with more powerful search tools than past researchers may have ever imagined. In the time it took them to formulate questions, you can search dozens of potential information sources. You belong to the first generation of college students to enjoy both quantity and quality in your research, along with a wider perspective on issues and the ability to form opinions after reasoning from a much wider knowledge base.

Certainly, the potential exists for the Internet to grind out a generation of intellectual robots who regurgitate information from many sources. Technology has always had its good and bad aspects; however, computer communications technology provides us the potential to become some of the best-informed thinkers in the history of the world. Aided by this technology, we may become thinkers who are not only articulate, but confident that our opinions have been distilled from a range of views and processed by our own personalities, beliefs, and biases. This is one of the aspects of the Internet that makes this era such an exciting combination of humanism and technology.

Criminology, Criminal Justice, and the Internet

The Internet has grown exponentially, and so have the number of Web sites devoted to criminology and criminal justice. Both of these

part
1

social sciences have a rapidly expanding knowledge base, vibrant professional organizations, numerous scholarly journals, hundreds of academic programs, and large student populations who identify themselves as criminology or criminal justice majors. Add to this the thousands of institutes, centers, think tanks, interest groups, government and private agencies, and it becomes easy to see why the Internet is the logical place to keep informed and expand your knowledge.

In the field of criminology and criminal justice today, the Internet is used primarily to disseminate information to the general public via Web sites. Through the Internet, agencies and organizations can inform the public about their goals and their operational structures. Agency Web sites usually include mission statements, personnel lists, press releases, annual reports, crime reports, fugitive lists, and crime prevention tips. More progressive agencies are experimenting with online forms for crime reporting, complaint handling, and job applications. A few have list servers where you can join in a discussion, and others have an email newsletter you can subscribe to for free. Most Web sites are accessible to the public, although there are a small number of restricted sites.

A handful of active newsgroups can be found on crime and justice topics, but few of these provide solidly useful information to the serious student of criminal justice. As for bulletin boards and chat rooms in this field, approximately 60 percent or more of these are closed to the general public; that is, the person must prove that they either work in law enforcement, have passed their state bar, or work in corrections. The chat rooms open to the general public are often concerned with one or more member's personal problems with the law, advice for writing a novel about crime, and/or someone peddling their personally developed training, self-defense, or personal safety materials—matters of little value to students. The criminology and criminal justice field has actually been somewhat slow to embrace Internet technology in such areas as distance education, training, interactivity, and collaboration, but that is rapidly changing. In the meantime, there is a wealth of informative Web sites.

Comprehensive Web Sites

As a student of criminology and criminal justice, you can use the Internet to explore any of several, large, comprehensive sites to get a complete overview of the field. Typically, these kinds of sites are put together by faculty in the field to assist students in their program and elsewhere around the world. You don't have to be enrolled at any particular school

part

1

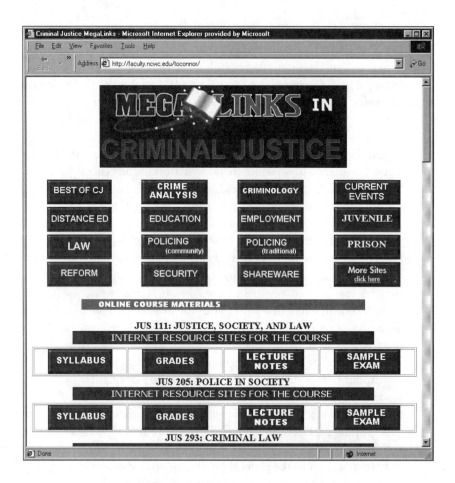

to take advantage of these sites. Visit MegaLinks in Criminal Justice (**http://faculty.ncwc.edu/toconnor**) to see such a site.

A good comprehensive site that arranges links by topic is Dr. Cecil Greek's Criminal Justice Links (**http://www.criminology.fsu.edu/cj.html**).

The Web sites of many institutes, interest groups, and nonprofit organizations will also have lengthy lists, or linklists, of the most popular and informative sites in criminology and criminal justice. Be warned, however, that the purpose of any site created for a cause will be to persuade as well as inform. Occasionally, one also runs into an excellent personal home page of a practitioner or student who has put together a fairly comprehensive collection of bookmarks and favorites in the field of criminology and criminal justice.

You can find just about anything you want at a comprehensive site. You'll enjoy just taking the time to explore them.

Specialized Web Sites

There are numerous specialized sites with valuable and scholarly information on popular topics in criminology and criminal justice. These kinds of sites make for useful references when researching a term paper or just learning more about a particular topic. Specialized Web sites can be easily found in such areas as child abuse, computer crime, crime prevention, death penalty, domestic violence, drug and alcohol use, gangs, gun control, hate crime, organized crime, pornography, restorative justice, juvenile justice, school violence, serial murder, sex offenders, terrorism, and victim's rights. For example, the American Bar Association, at last count, collected links to 500 juvenile justice Web sites.

There are, additionally, many news and newspaper sites that track the latest crime news, current events, and late-breaking headlines. *The New York Times* has a good online version that you can access by applying for

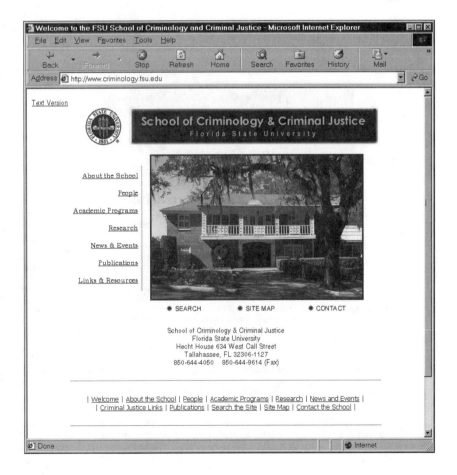

a free password. Most topical sites will contain essays, treatises, reports, and articles, and you can usually tell from the titles and the first few lines if the piece is objective and will be useful to you. In addition, nonprofit organizations and interest groups are usually devoted to a single cause, like victim's rights, or a specific sentencing reform. The Internet is the way these groups get the word out on what they do. The advantage of a guide like this is that it can provide you with a list of URLs to lead you to these hidden gems and keep you away from the less useful, sensationalistic sites.

Research Web Sites

Suppose you not only have to write a term paper, but you want or need to include some research, numbers, figures, or tables in it. Alternatively, suppose you just wanted to compare the crime rates or police salaries in

part

1

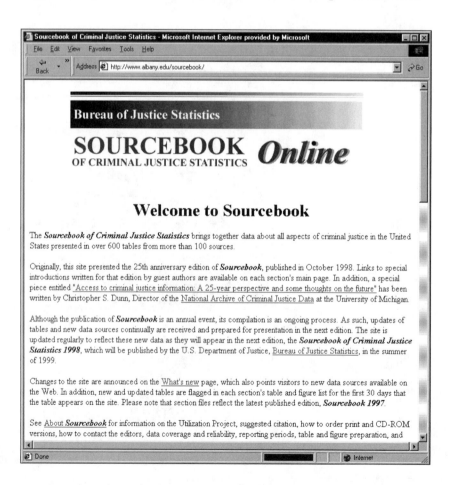

Houma, Louisiana with Dearborn, Michigan. Hands down, the Internet is the best way to do this, provided your browser has the free Adobe Acrobat Reader plug-in installed. All the latest crime and criminal justice data is available, either in raw form or already analyzed, and presented in neat, convenient tables—perfect for cut-and-paste operations into your term paper. (Remember, however, to include the appropriate documentation!)

Some examples would include the FBI's Uniform Crime Reports, which is a collection of city-by-city crime rates. Although the reporting program is voluntary, the rates are representative of 95 percent of the United States population. There's a two-year lag, however, in what the FBI releases to the general public. Tabular data as well as articles, bulletins, and other reports are also available at the Justice Information Center, a service of NCJRS (National Criminal Justice Reference Service), which is an information clearinghouse for many federal justice agencies. Both of these places are your source for official statistics.

Unfortunately, both the FBI and NCJRS Web sites are oriented primarily towards practitioners and policymakers. That doesn't mean a student wouldn't go there. It just means that grant writers, policy analysts, or agency administrators, for example, are the primary users of these sites for research data. Students, however, might find it more convenient to go to The Sourcebook of Criminal Justice Statistics (**http://www.albany.edu/sourcebook**). This site archives the most important data tables from many other sites.

The Sourcebook categorizes over 600 of the most-watched tables in criminology and criminal justice into six categories: (1) characteristics of the criminal justice system, such as employment levels, salaries, and so forth; (2) public opinion, about crime, drug use, and so forth; (3) nature and distribution of crime, or victimization data; (4) nature and distribution of persons arrested, or offender data; (5) judicial processing, or average sentences given out; and (6) persons under correctional supervision, such as probation, parole, or prison data. Other organizations with Web sites such as the Roper Center (**http://www.ropercenter.uconn.edu/**) or the Gallup organization (**http://www.gallup.com**) also generate public opinion data. In addition, each state maintains what is called an information authority, which acts as a clearinghouse for crime and justice data at the state level.

Law Web Sites

One area that is extremely important in criminology and criminal justice is the study of law. Law schools, centers, institutes, and law sites, in

part
1

general, have a big Internet presence, and the practice of legal research is almost done entirely by Internet these days. Suppose you want or need to look up the case of *Tennessee v. Garner* because your instructor keeps mentioning it. What you'll need is a good legal research search engine, and Findlaw (**http://www.findlaw.com**) fits the bill perfectly.

One of many excellent legal research sites, FindLaw is designed for a variety of audiences, including the general public. Internet sites about law are not just for lawyers anymore, and you wouldn't even recognize Cornell Law School's site as a law school because it's so user-friendly and geared for beginners. A few law sites are available by subscription only, but most of the public accessible ones have topical guides, bulletin boards, and even chat rooms. With a little practice at these user-friendly sites, you'll become a legal expert in no time and be able to keep up with the ever-changing law.

Agency Web Sites

These are the bedrock of the Internet in criminology and criminal justice. By exploring an agency's site, you will be able to tell what it is up to and what it has done lately. There are approximately 18,000 police agencies in the United States, roughly 17,000 courts, and about 4,500 prisons and jails, but don't expect every one of them to have a Web site. Still, we're talking about a lot of Web sites—especially in law enforcement. Not all of them have been collected yet; that is, there is no master list anywhere on the Internet. Agencies are posting their first Web sites every day. It takes search engines about a month to index a new site that is submitted, suggested, or found by them. Sometimes, a knowledgeable person in the agency creates an unofficial Web page, and then that Web page is later transferred to an official agency server. While there is no master index, one site that is quite large, very popular, and dedicated to policing is Officer.com (**http://www.officer.com**).

part

1

At Officer.com, you can browse through the nation's police depart-ment Web sites any way you want—geographically, by special operations, or by individual officer home pages. Look no further if you want to learn about specialized police units like air support, bomb squads, horse patrol, and SWAT teams. Of course, there are lots of other sites that index police departments by state, size, or employment opportunities, but Officer.com is the number one, most popular law enforcement site in the world. Ira Wilsker's Law Enforcement Sites on the Web (**http://www.ih2000.net/ira/ira.htm**) is a close second, and sites like Police Guide (**http://www.policeguide.com/**) are also pretty good. Finding a site that collects police agency links should be fairly easy to do, as there are many to choose from, each with its own way of organizing the links.

For the courts, there are a number of very good sites, but few of them that provide a comprehensive national listing. Since the United States operates under a dual court system, some sites specialize in collect-ing state court links and some specialize in the federal system. The same is true for corrections. There are only a couple of jails on the Internet, but you can easily find sites dedicated to corrections at the state level and corrections at the federal level.

One site that does a good job of keeping up with court sites, cor-rectional sites, and even probation and parole is the Web of Justice (**http://www.co.pinellas.fl.us/bcc/juscoord/explore.htm**).

Maintained by an information analyst out of Florida, the Web of Justice is unique in that it not only focuses on what other sites might skip over, like terrorism and weapons of mass destruction, but it indexes other comprehensive sites in criminology and criminal justice.

For corrections itself, go to the Corrections Connection (**http://www.corrections.com/**) for the largest source of online news and infor-mation in this area—especially if you want to follow the latest trends in training and privatization. The ground covered by corrections sites also includes gang research, inmate rights, racism, and the death penalty. As with all agency-related sites, don't be disappointed when you find they aren't as topical or informative as they ought to be. There are still a lot of agencies left that think the only proper use of the Internet is to post a mission statement and contact information. Hopefully, that will change soon.

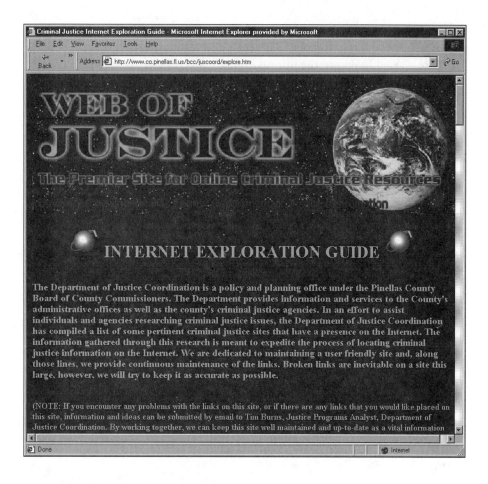

Employment Web Sites

Roughly 1,750,000 people earn their living by working in some capacity with the American criminal justice system. Some of them began their careers by surfing the Internet, and even by applying for a job online. Most of the federal agencies have hiring seasons in the late fall or early spring. In 1998, for example, the Border Patrol advertised for 1,000 new openings exclusively over the Internet. State civil service positions in almost every state can be viewed online, and the application forms can be downloaded in a variety of formats. There are also numerous employment help sites on the Internet for criminology and criminal justice. The point is: you can get a job online.

As you develop your interests and abilities in using the Internet, the skills you hone will be invaluable to your career, your agency, and concerned citizens in the communities of criminology and criminal justice. There is a real need for talent and fresh ideas in this area. People are needed to design the information architecture of justice-related Web sites, to improve communication with the public, to increase inter-agency cooperation, and to make whole systems more efficient and productive. Also, with new cybercrimes emerging, there is a need for professionals who can mix traditional methods with new technologies.

part

1

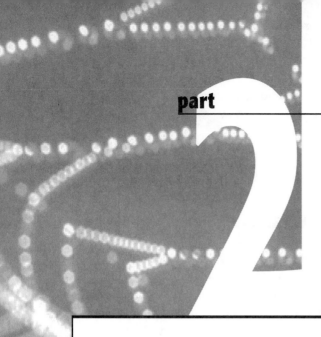

Activities in Criminology and Criminal Justice

In Part I we examined the variety of ways that the Internet has been used in criminology and criminal justice. We looked at comprehensive Web sites, specialized sites, research sites, law sites, agency sites, and job sites. This does not begin, however, to exhaust the endless possibilities for what the Internet can provide in the hands of a skillful Web surfer. In this section, therefore, we have prepared a series of activities to help you fine-tune your abilities at using the Internet in criminology and criminal justice.

Let's assume you are just beginning your career in criminology and criminal justice; that is, you're close to graduation and you want to start looking at ways to ply your trade or set up shop. Let's also assume you're interested in applying what you've learned in college, like the abilities to analyze crime, understand criminal offenders, and know how the criminal justice system is supposed to operate.

Think of these exercises, then, as routes or stages to a more productive and satisfying professional career. In fact, they do represent how a professional in criminology and criminal justice would use the Internet. Specifically, we will look at how you can use the Internet to accomplish the following objectives:

- Scan the latest crime news and headlines
- Review relevant criminological theories
- Check out what the think tanks think
- Agree or disagree with the ACLU

- Evaluate professional associations and their journals
- Get government grant money
- Take a stand on a crime bill
- Look for a better job

Scan the Latest Crime News and Headlines

One of the great benefits of the Internet is news gathering. You can literally read tomorrow's online edition of the news before the printed version hits the newsstands. Not only are there many excellent Internet sources for crime news, some sources even index the crime news from all the nation's newspapers for you.

1. Start your browser and go to **http://www.apbonline.com/**

2. Note how the Web site is organized. See if there are discussion forums, mailing lists, or chat rooms of interest to you, but focus on the crime stories and late-breaking news.

3. Go ahead and click on a few of the crime stories.

    Name two or three of the newspapers or other sources which apbonline.com relies upon in getting their stories.

    _____

    _____

    _____

    What types of crime does it seem that apbonline.com covers?

    _____

    _____

    _____

    From exploring the discussion forums and other features of this site, what occupations and interests do you think the participants have?

    _____

    _____

    _____

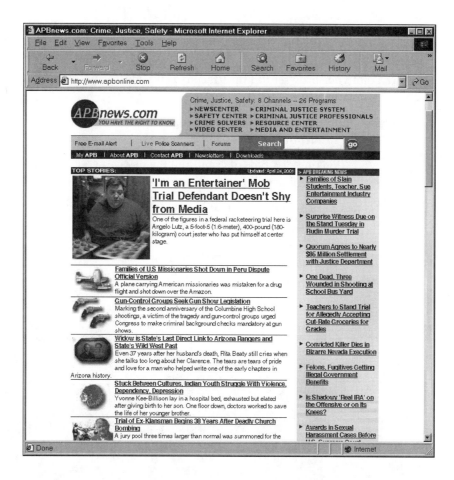

There are, of course, plenty of other Internet sources for crime news. Some people prefer sites like Cybersleuths.com (**http://www. cybersleuths.com/**) which are dedicated to unsolved cases. You should settle on your own favorite newspaper, magazine, or other source. There are two popular Mining Company guides on crime and justice, and the most active one is at **http://crime.about.com/**. Many people also rely upon the Drudge Report at **http://www.drudgereport.com** which allows you to scan the news wire services and read political commentary. Try to find a news source that is compatible with your interests and knowledge level.

Review Relevant Criminological Theories

New sites emerge all the time in this area, but the best sources currently are the comprehensive sites. Remember that these kinds of sites are typically put together by a faculty member for the benefit of their students and others around the Internet. There are several comprehensive sites in criminology and criminal justice to choose from.

1. Point your browser to **http://faculty.ncwc.edu/toconnor/ criminology.htm**

2. Scroll through the entire page without clicking on anything. Get a feel for the depth of content at a comprehensive site.

3. While thinking of a type of crime and the motives you suspect for it, read the two-column Table of Theory and Motives at this site.

   Name one or two theories that match up with the motives you suspect are the cause of the crime you have in mind.

   _____

   _____

   _____

part 2

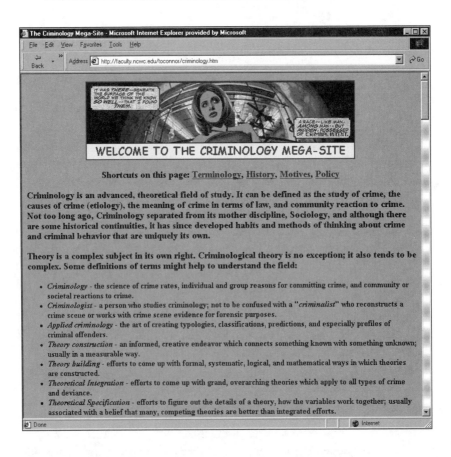

Now look at the Table of Policy Implications at this site. Which ones match up with the theory or theories you had in mind?

_____

_____

_____

One of the features of this site is the History of Criminology page. Go to it, and then do a word search or Find (on this Page) with your browser to locate books with titles that match the ideas in your theory. What books did you find?

_____

_____

_____

Other sites that are good comprehensive resources for criminological theory include the Redwood Highway (**http://www.sonoma.edu/cja/ info/infos.html**), Brendon J's Canadian Comprehensive Criminology (**http://www.pangea.ca/~cccl/**), and Cecil Greek's Criminal Justice Links (**http://www.criminology.fsu.edu/cj.html**). For strictly sociological theories, SocioRealm at **http://www.geocities.com/~sociorealm/** is your best bet, and for more biopsychological approaches, try CrimeTimes (**http://www.crime-times.org/**). You can also ask your instructor if he or she has a home page or a favorite site.

part

2

Check Out What the Think Tanks Think

There are numerous think tanks, research centers, institutes, and foundations in criminology and criminal justice. They have been extraordinarily influential in changing the shape of our justice system, as we know it. For example, our bail system would not be the same today if not for the Vera Institute (**http://broadway.vera.org/**), and we would not know as much as we do about detective work or the drug war without the Rand Corporation (**http://www.rand.org/**).

Some think tanks are affiliated with the government or a university, others are nonprofit organizations, and still others are philanthropic organizations. They invest lots of money into hiring the best talent and doing extensive research towards formulating policy papers on a wide range of issues. It is important you understand that think tanks are often supported by organizations with an ideological purpose; that is, they are usually progressive or conservative. You will find an inordinate number of them devoted to victim's rights, women's rights, children's rights, and drunk driving simply because these are areas which draw the most activism.

1. Point your browser to **http://www.policy.com/**

2. Take a moment to look over the opening page and see if there are any crime and justice issues highlighted by a special banner or button, but don't click on them right now.

3. Somewhere in the left margin there should be a lengthy table of contents. Scroll down until you see the words "Think Tanks," which may be under the heading of "Community." Click on "Think Tanks." You should see an alphabetical list of hundreds of think tanks.

part

2

Read the descriptions of the various think tanks (or perhaps do a word search or Find (on this Page) with your browser for words like "crime" and "justice"). Which think tanks are most directly relevant to criminology and criminal justice?

_____

_____

_____

Which think tanks are not directly relevant, but secondarily relevant, or connected with the root causes of crime or problems in criminal justice?

_____

_____

_____

For at least two of the think tanks, click on their links and view their home pages. Would you label them as progressive or conservative? Name the think tank and its ideological perspective.

_____

_____

_____

part

2

Most people can only keep track of a handful of think tanks. As you can see from their Web pages, these sites include an extensive amount of information. So, there's a real need for an indexing service like policy.com. Another site that many people find helpful is the Electronic Policy Network at **http://www.epn.org**—though it is more health and welfare oriented while policy.com is more crime and justice oriented. This should not matter much, however, since you're looking for reports on what is behind the crime problem, like broken homes or lack of employment opportunities.

Also, as you've discovered, it's difficult to tell which think tanks really have a direct relevance to criminology and criminal justice. You might find the site called Interest Groups in Criminal Justice (**http://faculty.ncwc.edu/toconnor/thnktank.htm**) helpful in this regard, as it lists the most relevant ones for you. Other good sites to search for expert opinion include the AAAS Directory of Human Rights Resources (**http://shr.aaas.org/dhr.htm**), the IGC JusticeNet (**http://www.igc.org**), John

Fuller's Peacemaking and Crime (**http://www.westga.edu/~jfuller/
peace.html**), and Critical Criminology's Home Page (**http://sun.soci.niu.
edu/~critcrim/**), although the latter two might require a bit of exploring.

Agree or Disagree with the ACLU

Welcome to the most powerful lobby group in criminology and criminal
justice, followed only by the ABA (**http://www.abanet.org/**) and perhaps
the NRA (**http://www.nra.org/**). The purpose of this exercise is to explore some of the resources on the ACLU home page and to develop
your critical judgment skills.

The American Civil Liberties Union was founded in 1920, about the
same time as the NAACP, and the two organizations have always worked
closely together, despite serious disagreements on matters such as the
ACLU's support of free speech rights for people espousing doctrines
of white supremacy. It's not that the ACLU supports white supremacy.
It's just that the ACLU will fight extremely hard to protect everyone's
constitutional rights to the fullest, including flag burning and other
controversial actions.

part

2

1. Point your browser to **http://www.aclu.org/**

2. Take a moment to look over any highlights of current events on the
    opening page and locate the table of contents, which should be in
    the right margin.

    On the opening page, what featured top stories are marked high
    priority, immediate alert, or otherwise suggesting the viewer take
    action? Do you think this is an effective attention-grabbing device?
    Did it make you feel empowered, or at least curious, that you could
    take action on something?

    _____

    _____

    _____

    In the table of contents, click on the words "criminal justice." Then,
    click on the main highlighted story on that page, and read the short
    essay. What is the ACLU's position? Do you support what they are
    recommending or do you think they are making too much out of it?

_____

_____

_____

Now, go back to the home page table of contents and click on the word "prisons." Read the short essay called Prisoners' Rights in a Free Society. Do you agree or disagree that more and more prisons are becoming unfit for human habitation?

_____

_____

_____

The ACLU is not the only place, of course, where you can exercise critical judgment or learn about individual rights. You might want to check out the UN High Commission on Human Rights (**http://www.**

unhchr.ch/), constitutional rights in other countries (**http://www.
uni-wuerzburg.de/law/index.html**), or Amnesty International (**http://
www.amnesty.org/**). It's often the case that a comparative perspective
provides a fresh way of looking at things. Many people regard the
Amnesty International's statement against the death penalty as the most
persuasive argument against it.

Evaluate Professional Associations and Their Journals

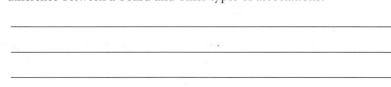
part
2

Let's assume the time has come in your professional career to join an
association of your peers. You know that doing so reflects credibility,
expertise, and some prestige upon yourself. You will have the chance
to attend conferences, present papers, win awards, gain recognition,
and have an outlet for your publications. This publication outlet would
usually be a journal subscription that comes free with your membership
subscription. Having a journal subscription also allows you to keep up
with the latest developments in your field. By the way, student member-
ships are usually available at a significantly reduced rate.

The question then becomes: which associations should you join?
Most people have limited budgets and can't join them all. What you
need is a Web site that lists the various associations and the journals
they provide. As of this printing, nothing like that which fits the bill
perfectly exists on the Internet, but a Web site that does list quite a few
associations is Frank Schmallenger's Cybrary.

1. Point your browser to **http://www.cjcentral.com/**

2. Click on the item marked "Dr. Frank Schmallenger's Criminal Justice
   Cybrary" and once this page loads, click on "Show All Categories".

3. Once the lengthy list of categories is seen, look for and click on the
   phrase "Associations in Criminal Justice". A lengthy list of professional associations should appear in your browser.

   Notice the names of the different associations. Some of them are called
   Boards and others are called Societies. Click on one or two examples of
   each. From reading their mission statements, does it seem like there's a
   difference between a board and other types of associations?

   _____

   _____

   _____

Find and click on the link for the American Board of Criminalistics. Explore everything on this site by clicking on anything provided: Overview, Examinations, Roster, Newsletter, and Information. What are the typical occupations of people who join this association? Does membership come with a journal subscription?

_____

_____

_____

Now, find and click on the American Society of Criminology. Read the online membership form. Are student rates available? Does membership come with a journal subscription?

_____

_____

_____

Since this exercise also involves evaluating online journals, go back to the main listing of associations, and click on different associations until you find one with an online newsletter or journal. Click on their newsletter or journal and read it. Do you find it directly relevant to criminology and criminal justice?

part

2

_____

_____

_____

This exercise makes the process of selecting a professional association more scientific than it has to be. Most people, in real life, join different groups on the basis of hit-and-miss or word-of-mouth. There is general agreement that the American Society of Criminology (**http://www.asc41.com/**) and the Academy of Criminal Justice Sciences (**http://www.acjs.org/**) are the top associations with the best journals at reduced student membership rates.

For your particular career interests, however, you may want to join a more specialized association—one dedicated to policing or private security, for example. To find out about these, you can visit any police megasite. A good starting place is The Best of CJ: Professional Organizations (**http://faculty.ncwc.edu/toconnor/linklist.htm#PROF**).

If you need help in determining the differences between a journal, a newsletter, a magazine, and a 'Zine, then check out Cornell University's Research Skills (**http://www.library.cornell.edu/okuref/research/skill20.html**) which distinguishes scholarly and non-scholarly periodicals.

Get Government Grant Money

Let's assume you've finally graduated from college and you're working at a famous research think tank or you've landed an entry-level managerial position in a justice or social service agency. Part of your job description may require that you write grants to receive government funding. More and more job descriptions are requiring the ability to obtain grants. The Internet is the best place to start developing that ability. In the field of criminology and criminal justice, there is no better place to begin the search for government grant money than the Justice Information Center, maintained by NCJRS, or the National Criminal Justice Reference Service.

1. Point your browser to **http://www.ncjrs.org/**

2. Ignore the fancy image map that shows up on the top of the page. Scroll down the page until you find and click on the button or words **Justice Grants.**

   How many individual Justice Department agencies provide funds to researchers? Are there any other agencies suggested on this page as possible places to look for federal grants? If so, what are they? Are there any grant announcements or solicitations that have been cancelled?

   _____

   _____

   _____

   Click on each of these individual agencies to see how the new address or URL changes in your browser. Which agencies take you to a completely different URL? What agencies offering grants provide the most information via their Web site?

   _____

   _____

   _____

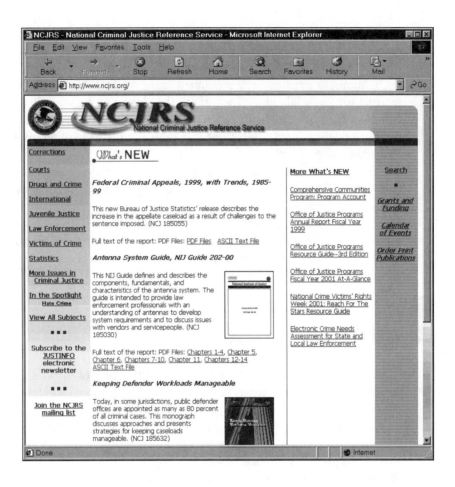

Look over the various grant opportunities at the individual agencies, either by reading the descriptions on the Justice Grants page or by exploring specific grant links themselves. From looking over the grant opportunities, are there any you could apply for where the deadline has not been reached?

_____

_____

_____

As this exercise made apparent, sometimes there are government agencies other than the Justice Department involved in grant opportunities for criminology and criminal justice. To look at the Web sites for these other agencies, you need a site like the Federal Web Locator (**http://www.infoctr.edu/fwl/**) or a site containing links to federal

part

2

agencies. Experienced researchers also have learned how to use the search engine for the Federal Register. This was presented to you on the Justice Grants page (**http://www.ncjrs.org/fedgrant.htm**).

Finding the appropriate government grant is a little like searching the Internet for financial aid. At least, that's the idea behind a site called the Community of Science (**http://www.cos.com/**) where you can find a section for undergraduate student research grants in the form of fellowships and scholarships.

State governments also have grant programs. Simply locate the home page for your state government and check their index, site map, or appropriate agency pages for grant opportunities. In addition, even though this exercise was focused on getting government grant money, you should not neglect looking into philanthropic organizations or private foundations. The Foundation Center (**http://fdncenter.org/**) is the gateway for private grants.

part

2

Take a Stand on a Crime Bill

Each year, hundreds of bills are introduced on the floor of the U.S. House or Senate. In this exercise, we will look at how you can easily locate a bill that relates to crime, any of your particular interests, or any proposed legislation that might affect the operations of the agency you work for. Whether or not you want to express a personal activism, it helps in almost all employment situations to stay on top of proposed legislation that might affect your area of work. You should also not hesitate to email your representative in Congress to take a stand. To do this, you need timely information on exactly how far a bill has progressed. If it has passed both houses of Congress, you may have to email the President.

1. Point your browser to **http://thomas.loc.gov/.**

2. Look for the input box that is Search Current Congress for Text of Bills, by Word/Phrase. Leave the box that says by Bill Number blank. Type the word "crime" in the by Word/Phrase box, and hit the search button.

   How many crime bills have been proposed in the current Congress, according to the results of your search? Look over this list of crime bills Exclude those that are not really crime bills, but changes in the tax code, creation of new holidays, etc. How many crime bills are there now?

_____

_____

_____

Go ahead and click on at least three crime bills that might interest you. The link to read the bill is usually located after its name in the form of a number, like S521 or HR2061. What are these crime bills about?

_____

_____

_____

For one of the bills that interest you, find out who introduced the bill, and what the disposition is. Who introduced the bill? What happened to the bill? Was it sent to committee, passed in one house but not the other, or passed and sent on to the President? Would you feel comfortable emailing a letter of support or opposition to the appropriate elected official?

part
2

_____

_____

_____

Look for a Better Job

Both salaries and cost of living vary widely in criminology and criminal justice, depending upon where you live in the country. A salary of $25,000 might get you by in some parts of the South, but it certainly won't pay the rent in New York City. What you need is an Internet guide to average salaries and cost of living. One particularly useful Web site is the Occupational Outlook Handbook (**http://www.umsl.edu/services/govdocs/ooh9899/1.htm**), which gives you information on salaries, work descriptions, qualifications, and growth trends; that is, whether your job is a dead-end or at least expected to grow moderately. This handbook is put together by economists, and some colleges even use it to plan which majors to offer. Another popular Web site is the Salary/Moving Calculators from HomeFair (**http://www2.homefair.com/calc/salcalc.html**). At this site, you plug in the name of the town you're thinking about moving to and your current address. You'll find out how much more or less you need to earn in order to afford your move. HomeFair can also calculate crime rate differences.

There are plenty of Internet employment guides in criminology and criminal justice. A few of them charge a subscription fee and others will constantly try to sell you booklets, but, by and large, the people who put together these guides have been pretty generous. This exercise will involve looking at one of these sites. It's free, regularly updated, and called Employment MegaLinks in Criminal Justice.

1. Point your browser to **http://faculty.ncwc.edu/toconnor/employ.htm.**

   Judging from the number of links available, what area of work (policing, courts, corrections, other) seems to be emphasized at this site? What area of work is neglected?

   _____

   _____

   _____

part

2

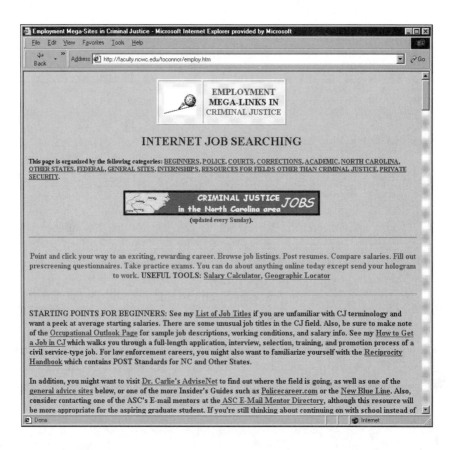

What does the phrase "open recruitment" mean? Indicate to what levels of government (local, county, state, or federal) this phrase applies.

_____

_____

_____

Good vocational guidance while you're still in college can be found at Dr. Carlie's AdviseNet (**http://courses.smsu.edu/mkc096f/**). For aspiring graduate students and professionals, the Email Mentoring Program of the American Society of Criminology (**http://sun.soci.niu.edu/ ~ascmentr/mentor.html**) matches your interests with an academic or practitioner who can give you sound professional advice.

Any of the megasites in criminology and criminal justice should have an employment advice or links page. One site that includes a unique collection of police links is Ira Wilsker's Law Enforcement Sites on the Web (**http://www.ih2000.net/ira/ira2.htm#jobs**).

part

2

List of URLs in Criminology and Criminal Justice

Criminology and Criminal Justice Megasites

Allyn and Bacon's Criminal Justice Links

`http://www.abacon.com/sociology/soclinks/cj.html`

An extensive collection of links to sites in victimology, policing, the courts and law, forensics, corrections, the death penalty, associations, and government and international organizations.

Charles Dreveskracht's Web site

`http://arapaho.nsuok.edu/~dreveskr/`

A site created by Professor Charles Dreveskracht at Northeastern State University with numerous links on topics in comparative criminology, victimology, criminal justice history, criminal justice research, and Native

American resources. The site also includes criminal justice education and career resources.

Crime Connections on the Web

http://www.justiceblind.com/links.html

A site created by Professor Matt Robinson at Appalachian State University with numerous links on topics in criminology, criminal justice, and government. The site also includes criminal justice education and drug links. This new location is organized around his book's format.

Crime Theory.com

http://www.crimetheory.com/

A site created by Professor Bruce Hoffman at the University of Washington with numerous links and original documents on the history, timeline, and major figures of criminology, including research topics, learning resources, and classroom assignments. The site is for both instructors and students, and also features a link of the month.

part

2

Criminal Justice Education Web

http://www.cjed.com/

A site created by Professor Philip Reichel at the University of Northern Colorado with numerous links on careers, research topics, writing, teaching, and classroom assignments. The site is for both instructors and students, and also contains correctional and international resources.

Criminal Justice Links

http://www.criminology.fsu.edu/cj.html

A site created by Professor Cecil Greek at Florida State University with numerous links arranged under topics in crime prevention, delinquency, drugs, law, obscenity, forensics, policing, the courts, corrections, international links, criminal justice education, crime in the media, criminal justice images and illustrations, and online criminal justice discussion groups and E-journals. The site also contains sample book chapters and a navigable map of the criminal justice system.

Criminal Justice MegaLinks

http://faculty.ncwc.edu/toconnor

A site created by Professor Tom O'Connor at North Carolina Wesleyan College with numerous links arranged by areas of interest in criminology, law, crime analysis, current events, juvenile justice, policing, prisons, system reform, computer security, criminal justice education, distance education, criminal justice technology, and criminal justice employment. The site also contains online lectures, sample exams, and a listing of the Best Sites in criminal justice.

Cybrary of Criminal Justice

http://talkjustice.com/cybrary.asp

A site created by Dr. Frank Schmalleger at the Justice Research Association with numerous links arranged in a Top 100 format and by categories and subcategories in criminal justice, criminology, law, criminal justice careers, criminal justice technology, discussion lists, journals, and 'Zines. The site also contains a glossary of criminal justice terms and a chat room.

JusticeLink (U.K.)

http://www.kcl.ac.uk/depsta/rel/ccjs/
justicelink/general.htm

A site created by Dr. Simon Marshall at the U.K. Centre for Crime and Justice Studies that contains many U.K. and U.S. links on criminology, law, policing, probation, prisons, criminology journals, international organizations, and international issues in criminal justice.

part

2

Law Enforcement Sites on the Web

http://www.ih2000.net/ira/ira.htm

A site created by Professor Ira Wilsker at Lamar University arranged by large pages of links on police departments, employment, domestic violence, forensics, drugs, corrections, law, the courts, and corrections. The site also contains terrorism links, computer crime links, and miscellaneous links.

Links to Criminal Justice Related Sites

http://cjwww.csustan.edu/cj/links.html

A site created by Professor Phyllis Gerstenfeld at California State University-Stanislaw with many links categorized by civil liberties, hate crimes, law enforcement, corrections, forensics, juvenile justice, law, social science, and politics.

Redwood Highway

http://www.sonoma.edu/cja/info/infos.html

A site created by Professor Pat Jackson at Sonoma State University with numerous links arranged by pages on criminology, law enforcement, law and the courts, corrections, special issues like the death penalty, system reform, international links, and electronic journals.

Web of Justice

http://www.co.pinellas.fl.us/bcc/juscoord/explore.htm

A site created by Tim Burns, an information analyst at the Pinellas County (FL) department of Justice Coordination with many links arranged by areas of interest in corrections, probation and parole, the courts, law enforcement, government, and international criminal justice.

Academic Sites

University of Alaska at Anchorage

http://www.uaa.alaska.edu/just/

The Justice Center at this school has an extremely comprehensive collection of links and online articles on issues of the death penalty, racism, human rights, victims, law enforcement, law, juvenile justice, the courts, and corrections. If you click on the icon for Introduction to American Justice, it's almost like an entire semester condensed into one Web page.

Arizona State University

http://www.asu.edu/copp/justice/

ASU's School of Justice Studies has extensive Internet resources on women's studies, Latino studies, alternative dispute resolution, mediation, fairness in media, and reform of drug laws.

University of Arkansas at Little Rock

http://www.ualr.edu/~cjdept/

This Department of Criminal Justice Web site has a list of honor societies in criminal justice, information about distance education, and links on corrections, human rights topics, law, policing, and computer technology.

California Lutheran University

http://robles.callutheran.edu/scj/scj.html

This Department of Criminal Justice has an extremely useful Web site with links categorized by corrections, gangs, criminal investigation, crime prevention, the courts, juvenile delinquency, law enforcement, law, sentencing, and substance abuse.

University of Delaware

http://www.udel.edu/soc/homepage.htm

part

2

This Department of Sociology and Criminal Justice houses the Disaster Research Center and a Center for Drug and Alcohol Studies.

Eastern Kentucky University

http://www.len.eku.edu/

This College of Law Enforcement Web site has links and online publications about community policing and public safety.

Florida Gulf Coast University

http://spss.fgcu.edu/cj/

This Division of Criminal Justice Web site contains links on associations, government, the courts, corrections, and juvenile justice.

Florida State University

http://www.criminology.fsu.edu/

FSU's School of Criminology and Criminal Justice has distance education information, affiliated associations, publications, links to various Police Corps nationwide, and the Criminal Justice Links site.

part

2

University of Illinois at Chicago

http://www.uic.edu/depts/cjus/

The UIC Department of Criminal Justice Web site has two notable institutes and centers on it. The Institute for Public Safety Partnership has extensive resources on community policing with multimedia clips. The Office of International Criminal Justice has online journals and archived documents.

Illinois State University

http://www.ilstu.edu/depts/cjs/

This Department of Criminal Justice Web site has resource pages on criminal justice history, rural crime, and drugs.

Indiana University of Pennsylvania

http://www.iup.edu/cr/

IUP's Department of Criminology has a research-oriented collection of links and online abstracts from the journal, Criminal Justice Policy Review.

John Jay College of Criminal Justice

http://www.jjay.cuny.edu/index.html

This college serves as a major research center for education and research in criminal justice, law enforcement, and forensic science.

University of Maryland

http://www.bsos.umd.edu/ccjs/

This college's Web site has information on technology, substance abuse, recidivism, and other research activities.

University of Memphis

http://www.people.memphis.edu/~cjustice/cjus.htm

This department's Web site has a rather unique resource directory on the topic of genocide, an interest of most of the faculty members.

Michigan State University

http://www.ssc.msu.edu/~cj/

MSU's School of Criminal Justice has online career information, distance education programs, and useful faculty member home pages.

University of Nebraska at Omaha

http://www.unomaha.edu/~crimjust/

This Department of Criminal Justice Web site has a list of links and houses a center for the study of community policing which has some information.

Northern Arizona University

http://www.nau.edu/~crimj-p/

This Department of Criminal Justice Web site has some good faculty member home pages and a prelaw page that helps you decide if going to law school is the right idea.

Pennsylvania State University

http://www.la.psu.edu/admj/welcome.htm

PSU's Program in Crime, Law, and Justice has a Web site that contains a link under Other Sites of Interest to their school's library page which is a megasite for the topics of delinquency, victimization, and sentencing.

Portland State University

http://www.upa.pdx.edu/AJ/

This Division of Administration of Justice has an extensive set of criminal justice links on the topics of law enforcement, law, news, and guns.

Rutgers, the State University of New Jersey

http://rutgers-newark.rutgers.edu/rscj/

This School of Criminal Justice Web site has a good collection of links on corrections and the courts. It also houses a Center for Crime Prevention, the World Criminal Justice Library Network, and the NCCD (National Council on Crime and Delinquency) collection of monographs and dissertations.

Sam Houston State University

http://www.shsu.edu/cjcenter/

This site is really three sites in one. There's the College of Criminal Justice, a Law Enforcement Institute, and a Corrections Institute. Each one has extensive criminal justice links and some online publications.

San Jose State University

http://www.sjsu.edu/depts/casa/aj/index.html

This Department of Administration of Justice has a small, but good, collection of links on human rights, corrections, law enforcement, forensics, and juvenile justice. Click on the tab for Misc. to get to the links.

University of South Carolina

http://www.sc.edu/crju/

This college has a small, but good collection of links on law enforcement, corrections, courts, victimology, and firearms.

Southern Illinois University

http://www.siu.edu/~ajsiuc/

This Department of Administration of Justice has a Web page on crime mapping and how to read a map.

Southwest Texas State University

http://www.cj.swt.edu/

This department's Web site has a well-organized collection of Internet resources on policing, courts, corrections, probation, and parole.

part
2

State University of New York at Albany

`http://www.albany.edu/scj/`

SUNY-Albany's School of Criminal Justice Web site has some career information, faculty home pages, and extensive links on law, the courts, corrections, the death penalty, drugs, and victims. It also houses the Sourcebook of Criminal Justice Statistics and the Journal of Criminal Justice and Popular Culture.

Temple University

`http://www.temple.edu/cjus/`

This Department of Criminal Justice Web site has a couple of excellent faculty member home pages with resources on white-collar crime, hate crime, sentencing, race and crime, and drugs.

University of Southern Mississippi

`http://www.cj.usm.edu/`

This Department of Criminal Justice Web site has a collection of links on family and juvenile studies, policing, corrections, law, and a link to Adam McKee's criminal justice page, which is a separate resource in itself.

part

2

Government Resources

Alcohol, Tobacco and Firearms

`http://www.atf.treas.gov/`

A Treasury Department bureau charged with reducing crime, collecting revenue, and protecting the public. It also investigates explosions, bombings, and arsons.

Border Patrol

`http://www.ins.usdoj.gov/graphics/lawenfor/index.htm`

A branch of the Justice Department's Immigration and Naturalization Service charged with enforcement of the immigration laws.

Bureau of Prisons

`http://www.bop.gov/`

The U.S. Bureau of Prisons manages ninety-four federal prisons at all levels of security. Their Web site offers information on their prisoners, employment information, and other facts.

Customs

http://www.customs.ustreas.gov/

The U.S. Customs Service is charged with ensuring lawful trade and travel.

Drug Enforcement Administration

http://www.usdoj.gov/dea/

A Justice Department agency charged with enforcement of all controlled substances in the United States.

Federal Bureau of Investigation

http://www.fbi.gov/

A Justice Department agency with a broad mandate to investigate all other crimes not assigned to any other federal agency.

Federal Judicial Center

http://www.fjc.gov/

This site is the home page of the research and continuing education wing for the federal courts, and the site consists of downloadable publications covering a wide range of topics, from sentencing guidelines to information about habeas corpus writs.

Federal Judiciary Home Page

http://www.uscourts.gov/

This is a site set up for the general public to assist in understanding of how court systems operate. Their publication, "About the U.S. Courts," is excellent, and the site covers both state and federal court systems.

FedWorld

http://www.fedworld.gov

A site that offers quick access to thousands of United States government Web sites, online government documents, databases, and other information.

House of Representatives

http://www.house.gov

A quick and easy way to locate and contact your representative.

part
2

Library of Congress

http://lcweb.loc.gov

Online resources that are considered useful to the American people and to sustain and preserve a universal collection of knowledge for future generations. Contains topical and historical collections as well as other featured exhibitions.

National Archive of Criminal Justice Data

http://www.icpsr.umich.edu/NACJD/

Large, downloadable datasets that have been deposited by government-funded researchers in hopes that someone else can "mine" the data through secondary analysis and extract more conclusions than the original researchers did.

National Clearinghouse on Child Abuse and Neglect

http://www.calib.com/nccanch/

Funded by the Children's Bureau, this organization acts as an information resource for people seeking information on prevention, identification, and treatment of child abuse and neglect.

National Consortium for Justice Information and Statistics

http://www.search.org/

Funded by the government, this organization conducts symposiums and conferences designed to improve the information gathering and dissemination functions of justice agencies. It acts as a clearinghouse of information on the latest software solutions, maintains a shareware library, and produces some publications.

National Crime Victimization Survey (NCVS)

http://www.ojp.usdoj.gov/bjs/cvict.htm

This site is one of the major sources of crime data in the form of victim surveys. The survey results are usually portrayed as the number of households touched by crime.

National Criminal Justice Reference Service

http://www.ncjrs.org/

The most extensive resource of information of criminal and juvenile justice in the world. NCJRS is a collection of clearinghouses supporting all bureaus of the Department of Justice, Office of Justice Programs, the National Institute of Justice, the Office of Juvenile Justice and Delin-

part

2

quency Prevention, the Bureau of Justice Statistics, the Bureau of Justice Assistance, and the Office for Victims of Crime. It also supports the Office of National Drug Control Policy.

National Incident-Based Reporting System (NIBRS)

http://www.nibrs.search.org/

This is a home page of the NIBRS project which will eventually replace the Uniform Crime Report (UCR) format that the FBI presently uses.

National Institute of Corrections

http://www.nicic.org/inst/

Funded by the Justice Department and technically part of the Bureau of Prisons, the NIC provides training programs in corrections and carries out objective research on corrections. Their Web site offers a collection of prison-related Internet resources as well as access to some of their own publications.

National Law Enforcement and Corrections Technology Center

part

2

http://www.nlectc.org/

An exhaustive resource of information on currently used and soon-to-be-developed crime-fighting technology. The site maintains a database of less-than-lethal weaponry, protective equipment, and surveillance devices in various stages of commercialization and development. It also provides updates on the forensic uses of DNA and crime mapping technology.

Senate Home Page

http://www.senate.gov/

A quick and easy way to locate and contact your senator.

Sourcebook of Criminal Justice Statistics

http://www.albany.edu/sourcebook/

Funded by the Justice Department, the Sourcebook contains over 600 of the most important tables of numbers on characteristics of the criminal justice system, characteristics of criminal offenders, and public opinion about crime and the criminal justice system.

Thomas—U.S. Congress on the Internet

http://thomas.loc.gov/

Access to the latest crime bills, laws, Congressional Record, reports, and links to further information.

Uniform Crime Reports (UCR)

http://www.fbi.gov/ucr.htm

The official crime rates for the United States, available for viewing.

United Nations Crime and Justice Information Network

http://www.uncjin.org

Extensive information on international crimes like money laundering, bribery, and corruption.

U.S. Attorney's Manual

http://www.usdoj.gov/usao/eousa/
foia_reading_room/usam/

This site details exactly what a United States attorney is supposed to do, how to act, and how to function. The site also explains the role of a prosecutor.

U.S. Department of Justice

http://www.usdoj.gov/

Cabinet-level agency consisting of many branches, including the FBI and DEA, who are charged with enforcement of all federal crimes.

U.S. Intelligence Community

http://www.odci.gov/ic/

A group of about thirteen agencies, including the CIA, who are charged with defending the national security.

U.S. Marshals

http://www.usdoj.gov/marshals/

A Service within the Justice Department that is responsible for protecting the judiciary, federal witnesses, transporting federal prisoners, and managing seized assets.

U.S. Parole Commission

http://www.usdoj.gov/uspc/

A bureau within the Justice Department that sets policy and conditions affecting federal parolees and the work of federal probation and parole officers. Their site has a rather lengthy document explaining how the parole system works.

part
2

U.S. Postal Inspectors

http://www.usps.gov/websites/depart/inspect/

A federal agency charged with enforcing a variety of crimes, like blackmail, mail fraud, child pornography, and counterfeiting.

U.S. Sentencing Commission

http://www.ussc.gov/

An informative site with many guidelines on various aspects of sentencing, including trends, issues, and the ongoing movement towards guidelines.

White House Social Statistics Briefing Room

http://www.whitehouse.gov/fsbr/crime.html

This site is what the President's office uses to keep track of various crime summaries.

Professional Associations

part

2

Academy of Criminal Justice Sciences

http://www.acjs.org/

The ACJS is one of the premier associations for criminal justice educators and professionals. The site maintains links to its regional associations, and provides a set of links to various Internet resources such as criminal justice related newsletters, mailing lists, and Web pages of its members.

American Academy of Forensic Sciences

http://www.aafs.org/

The AAFS consists of scientists, lawyers, physicians, criminalists, toxicologists, dentists, physical anthropologists, document examiners, engineers, psychiatrists, and educators with an interest in forensic science. Their Web site contains career information and links of interest.

American Bar Association

http://www.abanet.org/

An association for lawyers and law students, the ABA Web site has extensive online resources for the general public on law, domestic violence, homelessness, drugs, and juvenile justice.

American Board of Criminalistics

http://www.criminalistics.com/

The ABC is an organization of forensic scientists that are involved in work requiring board certification. This site has a list of graduate programs in forensic science.

American Judicature Society

http://www.ajs.org/

This is an association of judges. Their Web site has extensive resources on judicial selection, judicial conduct, judicial independence, and other issues of importance to judges.

American Psychiatric Association

http://www.psych.org/

A medical specialty society with over 40,000 members specialized in the diagnosis and treatment of mental and emotional illness and substance use disorders.

part

2

American Society of Criminology

http://www.asc41.com/

The ASC is one of the premier associations for criminology and criminal justice educators and professionals. The site maintains links to its divisions, employment listings, and other sites of interest to criminologists.

American Society for Industrial Security

http://www.asisonline.org/

ASIS is the premier association for private security professionals. Their extensive Web site provides information about careers, news of interest to security and protection professionals, and other items.

Association for Crime Scene Reconstruction

http://www.acsr.com/

ACSR is a group of investigators, forensic experts, and teachers who work on the development and study of deductive and inductive reasoning skills in drawing inferences from crime scene evidence. Their site contains a Test Your Crime Scene Knowledge quiz.

British Society of Criminology

http://www.lboro.ac.uk/departments/ss/BSC/homepage/
HOMEPAGE.HTM

This association's Web site has information about the society, workshops, seminars, ways to stay in touch with its six branches, links of interest, and a Web journal.

High Technology Crime Investigation Association

http://htcia.org

HTCIA is a group of investigators who study the special techniques necessary for dealing with crimes involving technology more advanced than traditional techniques or departments can handle.

International Association of Chiefs of Police

http://www.theiacp.org/

This premier law enforcement association Web site has quite a bit of information arranged alphabetically by topic. Sample topics include the police response to domestic violence and their legislative agenda.

part 2

International Association of Correctional Officers

http://www.oicj.org/public/

This site is home to "The Keeper's Voice," an online newsletter, and contains information, news, and articles on prison life, prison programs, and prisoner rights.

International Association of Directors of Law Enforcement Standards and Training

http://www.iadlest.org/

IADLEST is an association of training managers involved in the training of law enforcement officers. Their site contains a state member directory which is a list of links to every police officer certification authority nationwide.

International Association for Identification

http://www.theiai.org

This is a law enforcement association consisting mostly of crime scene investigators and crime lab workers. Their Web site has extensive resources on various forensic techniques, such as fingerprinting and forensic art, as well as numerous other links to resources on the Internet or on their site.

International Association of Police Planners

http://www.ialep.org/

IAPP is an association of police executive staff who network and share common interests. Their Web site contains reports from their meetings, other important announcements, and links of interest to their members.

International Association of Women Police

http://www.iawp.org/

This association Web site has tons of information, including related links, on the policewomen's movement and an online magazine.

International Community Corrections Association

http://www.iccaweb.org/

The site contains information about the history of halfway houses and how the community corrections movement has grown today.

National Criminal Justice Association

http://www.sso.org/ncja/

A group in Washington, D.C. that represents state and local governments to lobby for more effective crime control legislation. They produce a series of monthly and quarterly publications, some of which can be viewed from their Web site.

National Drug Enforcement Officers Association

http://www.ndeoa.org/

NDEOA is a group of law enforcement officers who work or have an interest in drug enforcement. Their Web site contains information about meeting announcements and links of interest.

National Legal Aid and Defender Association

http://www.nlada.org/d-perform.htm

This site contains a set of performance standards that defense lawyers are judged by. There is also information on the general duties and functions of defense lawyers.

part

2

National Organization of Black Law Enforcement Executives

http://www.noblenatl.org/

NOBLE is the premier law enforcement organization for African Americans. Their site is news-oriented and contains information on scholarship and grant opportunities.

National Association of Blacks in Criminal Justice

http://www.nabcj.org/

NABCJ is an association of African Americans working in the criminal justice system; as police, in the courts, or in corrections. Their Web site has a newsletter, meeting announcements, and links of interest.

National Sheriffs Association

http://www.sheriffs.org/

A group dedicated to furthering professionalism and sharing ideas in criminal justice.

Police Executive Research Forum

http://www.policeforum.org/

PERF is one of the premier associations in criminal justice, based on the idea that academics and police executives can work together to devise innovative, creative changes. Their Web site contains sample publications, downloadable databases, and a collection of Internet resources.

Society for Police and Criminal Psychology

http://www.jmu.edu/psyc/spcp/

SPCP is an association of academics and professionals with an interest in all aspects of psychology applied to the criminal justice system. Their Web site contains information about their meetings, a diplomate program, and a list of forensic psychology graduate programs.

Society of Police Futurists International

http://www.policefuturists.org/

This association consists of academics and professionals who have an interest in futurism and futurist studies, and how those long-range forecasts have implications for practical criminal justice work. Their Web site consists of issue papers, links of interest, and membership information.

part

2

Specialty Areas

COMPUTER CRIME

Center for Democracy and Technology

http://www.cdt.org/

A news-oriented site that focuses upon encryption and other government initiatives related to ensuring a future of safer computing.

Cnet's Finest: How Law Enforcement Cracks Down on Computer Crime

http://www.cnet.com/Content/Features/Dlife/Finest/

A story about police sting operations.

part

2

Computer Crime Research Resources

http://mailer.fsu.edu/~btf1553/ccrr/welcome.htm

An incredibly resourceful page created by an FSU grad student.

Criminal Justice MegaLinks: Sources of Information on People

http://faculty.ncwc.edu/toconnor/sources.htm

A Web page with links on computer security and computerized databases and how investigators can find out information about anyone.

Cybercrimes

http://www.cybercrimes.net/

An informative site from the University of Dayton Law School.

Electronic Frontier Foundation

http://www.eff.org/

One of the most influential sites on the Internet, it discusses the future of Internet technology and its many promises and pitfalls. Contains special features on government-driven hacker crackdowns.

International Association of Computer Investigative Specialists

http://cops.org/

This is an extensive site produced by an international volunteer nonprofit corporation composed of law enforcement professionals dedicated to education in the field of forensic computer science.

PedoWatch

```
http://www.pedowatch.org/leinfo/
```

A citizen safety-oriented comprehensive site on pedophilia and Internet child pornography.

WebGator: Investigative Resources on the Internet

```
http://www.inil.com/users/dguss/wgator.htm
```

A site set up by a private investigator with extensive resources for finding anybody.

CORRECTIONS

AZ Prison Reform Committee

```
http://www.eaznet.com/~jet/
```

A prison reform site with articles and links on aspects of inmate life, such as the inmate diet and overcrowding.

part
2

Behind the Walls

```
http://home.msen.com/~sky1/
```

A site put together by a correctional officer in Michigan which deals with controversial issues in corrections, like homosexuality, pepper spray, and privatization. The site also maintains a collection of Internet resources.

Black Peoples' Prison Survival Guide

```
http://www.cs.oberlin.edu/students/pjaques/etext/
prison-guide.html
```

A Web site featuring an essay written by an ex-convict that claims to tell it like it is about prison and how to survive in it.

Bob Brandoff's Cyber Cellblock

```
http://www.bestweb.net/~bobby375/
```

A site created by a correctional officer which documents his personal career history and offers a multimedia tour of a prison with his commentary along the way.

Correctional Officer's Information Page

http://www.geocities.com/MotorCity/Downs/3548/
index.html

A site created by a New York State correctional officer which provides a
tremendous number of Internet links on many different correctional topics, specifically issues affecting the unionization of correctional officers.

Corrections Connection Network

http://www.corrections.com/

The largest site on the Internet devoted to corrections with vast resources
on the topics of technology, education, healthcare, and privatization. It
also houses the main prison work professional associations, the American
Correctional Association and the American Jail Association.

Corrections/Law Enforcement Connection

http://members.aol.com/KPRIOR1869/index.html

An AOL home page put together by a correctional sergeant in California
that indexes other correctional officer home pages around the nation.
The site also offers a multimedia tour of a California prison, other
correctional links, miscellaneous links, and a police links page.

Corrections Education Connection

http://www.io.com/~ellie/

This site provides detailed content on any and all areas affecting the
success of education in corrections. There are extensive Internet resources
categorized by substance abuse problems, family problems, prison culture
problems, health problems, political problems, and the learning difficul-
ties of inmates.

Criminal Justice Links: Community Corrections and Prisons

http://www.fsu.edu/~crimdo/prison.html

Part of a comprehensive site that provides links for community based
correctional organizations, community courts, alternative dispute resolution, prison commissions, prison history, prison reform, and death
penalty links.

Criminal Justice MegaLinks: Prison
and Prison-Related MegaLinks

http://faculty.ncwc.edu/toconnor/prison.htm

**part
2**

Part of a comprehensive site that provides links to the Web sites for the prison systems of all fifty states, some federal prisons, and the larger metropolitan jails. Related Internet resources are also listed.

Division of Critical Criminology's Prison Information and Papers

`http://sun.soci.niu.edu/~critcrim/`

An extensive collection of links and original papers on prisons, prison issues, women in prison, prison culture, and prison statistics.

Eastern State Penitentiary

`http://www.libertynet.org/~e-state/`

This is a site that documents the history of the Pennsylvania style penitentiaries in the United States.

History of the North Carolina Prison System

`http://www.doc.state.nc.us/admin/page1.htm`

This site is part of a two-part series of historic photos and commentary showing how the state's prison system evolved from all the way back when prisoners were toted around in horse-drawn cages.

part

2

JailNet

`http://www.jail.net/`

A site with links and resources on issues affecting jail administration, including the law and mandatory jail services. There is a state-by-state directory of jail links.

Jeremy Bentham's Panopticon

`http://www.bestweb.net/~bobby/375/home12.htm`

This sites explains in both photos and words what Bentham's Panopticon prison's design looked like and was all about.

New Jersey State Parole Board

`http://www.state.nj.us/parole/`

This site does a good job of explaining the philosophy and operations of a parole board.

New York City Department of Corrections

`http://www.ci.nyc.ny.us/html/doc/`

The Web site for a system of municipal jails that holds more inmates than some state systems. The site contains history information, archived information, and online newsletters.

New York State Probation Officers Association

http://www.nyspoa.com/

This site does a good job of explaining what a probation officer does.

Penal Lexicon

http://www.penlex.org.uk/

Based in the United Kingdom and, although offering a paid subscription-only newsletter, the site offers a large collection of Internet resource links, especially in the area of rehabilitation.

Prison Issues Desk

http://www.prisonactivist.org/

A site by the Prison Activist Resource Center which contains excellent original resources on the prison crisis, prison law, women prisoners, political prisoners, and prison reform and/or abolition.

Prison Law Page

http://www.wco.com/~aerick/

An informative site dealing with correctional law, inmate rights, the death penalty, and inmate perspectives. The site contains a vocabulary guide to prisoner lingo or jargon as well as a number of other essays and articles.

Prisons.com

http://www.prisons.com/

A site which features the latest industry products in corrections. It also hosts the online magazine, *Corrections Forum*.

Private Prisons

http://www.ucc.uconn.edu/~logan/

A site put together by a University of Connecticut professor which provides both sides of argument in the privatization of prisons debate.

Web of Justice: Corrections-Related Links

http://www.co.pinellas.fl.us/bcc/juscoord/
ecorrections.htm

Part of a mega-site with a lengthy list of alphabetized Internet resources in corrections. State links are mixed in the list with other links.

Web of Justice: Probation and Parole Links

`http://www.co.pinellas.fl.us/bcc/juscoord/`
`eprobation.htm`

Part of a mega-site with a lengthy list of Internet resources in probation and parole. The list is alphabetized by state, but not all states are represented.

COURTS

Administrative Offices of the U.S. Courts

`http://www.uscourts.gov/`

An exhaustive amount of information on the federal court system.

ADR and Mediation Links

`http://adrr.com/`

This is a very extensive site on all things related to alternative dispute resolution and mediations, from its philosophy to its actual operations. The site features a topical guide and online essays.

part
2

American Judges Association

`http://www.ncsc.dni.us/aja/`

A central clearinghouse of information designed to assist judges and judicial staff. The AJA offers conferences, seminars, and research resources for its member.

Courtroom 21

`http://www.courtroom21.net/`

A site at College of William and Mary demonstrating the advantages of technology-augmented adjudication and modern courtrooms.

Federal Court Finder

`http://www.law.emory.edu/FEDCTS/`

An excellent guide to the federal court system from Emory University Law School.

Gwinnett Judicial Circuit

`http://www.courts.co.gwinnett.ga.us/`

This site in Georgia gives a great overview of superior courts and courts of limited jurisdiction.

Law and Court-Related Web sites

http://www.ncsc.dni.us/court/sites/lawsites.htm

This site includes links to legal institutions of all kinds, including courts, law schools, law libraries, governments, legislatures, and law firms. It is an excellent starting point for researching the judicial process.

National Association for Court Management

http://www.nacmnet.org/

This site includes links to court-related Web sites, an online newsletter, and other publications on how to more effectively manage the courts to improve public access to them.

National Center for the State Courts

http://www.ncsc.dni.us/

An exhaustive amount of information on state court systems.

Oyez Oyez Oyez

http://oyez.nwu.edu/

This is a multimedia-enriched site with excellent information about the U.S. Supreme Court. It also briefs key cases and analyzes oral arguments.

Redwood Highway: Law and Court Links

http://www.sonoma.edu/cja/info/infop3.html

Part of a mega-site with an annotated guide to legal sites. The bottom of the page focuses exclusively on California.

Serious Criminal Defense Litigation

http://www.execpc.com/~wrfincke/

A seasoned lawyer tells it like it is about defending clients. The site defines the role of the lawyer, the adversarial system, and more.

State Justice Institute

http://www.statejustice.org/

The SJI award grants to improve the quality of justice in the state court systems facilitate better coordination and information sharing, and to foster innovative, efficient solutions to common problems faced by all courts.

CRIME ANALYSIS
Crime Mapping and Analysis

```
http://everest.hunter.cuny.edu/capse/projects/
nij/crime.html
```

This is a site put together by a government researcher to post the results of his research. The result is a site that offers practical explanations and suggestions for getting started with GIS or geographic mapping.

Criminal Justice MegaLinks: Data Sources in Criminal Justice

```
http://faculty.ncwc.edu/toconnor/data.htm
```

A site put together by a college professor for students to learn about how and where to collect crime-related data, arranged by topic.

International Association of Crime Analysts

```
http://www.iaca.net/
```

This association has an extensive and useful Web site. The site includes tutorials on crime mapping, what crime analysis is, a list of job openings, a newsletter, and related links of interest.

Tempe (AZ) Police Department Crime Analysis Unit

```
http://www.tempe.gov/cau/default.htm
```

Informative site about police analysis of crime data.

CRIME LABS AND FORENSIC SCIENCE
Anil Aggrawal's Forensic Toxicology Page

```
http://members.tripod.com/~Prof_Anil_Aggrawal/
```

This is an interesting site from India on various topics in forensic medicine, with links to other Internet resources. It contains an online journal.

Carpenter's Forensic Science Links

```
http://www.tncrimlaw.com/forensic/
```

This extensive site offers excellent resources in forensic anthropology, pathology, entomology, odontology, document examination, and crime scene investigation. There's also information on education in forensic science.

part
2

Forensic Psychiatry and Medicine

http://www.forensic-psych.com/articles/
catCrimJust.html

This site contains excellent articles on the evidentiary rules of forensic science, as well as explaining the difference between diminished capacity defenses and insanity defenses.

Forensic Psychiatry Resource Page

http://bama.ua.edu/~jhooper/

A large and useful site on the variety of services offered by a psychologist or psychiatrist in law. It explains a bit about getting at the *mens rea* requirement.

Forensic Resource and Criminal Law Search Site

http://www.kruglaw.com/

A large and extremely useful site with over 900 forensic science, criminal law, and death penalty resources.

Fraud Detection

http://haven.ios.com/~nyrc/new33.htm

Links to and about the whole areas of lie detection, document examination, handwriting analysis, and fraud detection.

Knowledge Solutions

http://www.corpus-delicti.com/

A site that sells online courses in forensic science and psychological profiling. Some of the content is free, however, and the resources are quite good. Topics include computer crime and serial killing.

Michigan State Police Forensic Science Division

http://members.aol.com/stevenkl/fsdhome2.htm

A well-done page with exhaustive depth of content in DNA fingerprinting, ballistics, and other topics. It also contains links to other forensic crime labs around the country.

Reddy's Forensic Science Links

http://haven.ios.com/~nyrc/homepage.html

This is one of the premier forensic science sites on the Internet. It has dozens of pages on just about any kind of forensic science imaginable.

Reference Manual on Scientific Evidence

`http://www.fjc.gov/EVIDENCE/science/sc_ev_sec.html`

A lengthy and detailed account of the evidentiary standards for all the different types of forensic science from federal government guidelines.

Study Guides in Forensic Science

`http://www.msu.edu/user/siegelj/`

Study guides and notes provided online by a Michigan State University professor.

Zeno's Forensic Page

`http://forensic.to/forensic.html`

This is one of the premier forensic science sites on the Internet. Although all types of forensic science are represented, the site concentrates on medical, psychiatric, and psychological specialties.

CRIME NEWS

About.com: Current Events—Civil Liberties

`http://civilliberty.about.com/newsissues/civilliberty/`

A site that "mines" the Internet for the best stories about civil liberties.

About.com: Current Events—Crime/Punishment

`http://crime.about.com/newsissues/crime/`

A site that "mines" the Internet for the best stories about crime.

About.com: Current Events—Law

`http://law.about.com/newsissues/law/`

A site that "mines" the Internet for the best stories about law.

APB Online

`http://www.apbonline.com/`

A multimedia site devoted mainly to the unsolved crimes genre.

Constitutional Law News

`http://www.ljx.com/practice/constitutional/index.html`

A site that brings you the latest decisions from the Supreme Court. It also tracks cases before they get to the Supreme Court.

part
2

Court TV Online

http://www.courttv.com/

An extensively resourceful site that focuses upon the latest trials, crime stories, and pros and cons.

Criminal Justice MegaLinks: Current Events

http://faculty.ncwc.edu/toconnor/current.htm

A site put together by a college professor with links to the top news stories arranged in an alphabetical list of topics.

CyberSleuth's Crime News

http://www.cybersleuths.com/

A site that scans the nation's newspapers for top stories.

Policy News

http://www.policy.com/

A late-breaking news site that focuses on events and decisions with important policy implications.

Stupid People, Crime, and Current Events

http://www.mindspring.com/~iam392/

A rather amusing yet serious site covering stories and news items and also discussing issues like police use of force and liability.

Yahoo's Full Coverage of Prison News

http://headlines.yahoo.com/Full_Coverage/US/Prisons/

A site that indexes all the latest news in corrections, such as escapes, riots, lawsuit settlements, and significant changes in legislation affecting prison administration or prisoners.

CRIME PREVENTION

Community Watch Project

http://www.blockclubs.org/

This site has extensive resources on how communities, specifically community block watches, fight prostitution, crack houses, youth truancy and violence, graffiti, and more.

part

2

National Crime Prevention Council

http://www.ncpc.org/

Home of McGruff the Crime Dog and other resources on crime prevention.

Security Management Online

http://www.securitymanagement.com/

An online magazine and extensive resource site on the many areas of private security.

CRIMINAL JUSTICE EDUCATION

Complete Criminal Justice, Criminology, and Criminal Law Glossary

http://talkjustice.com/files/glossary.htm

This site contains every possible term you would need to know in criminology and criminal justice. The searchable database gives the definitions of over 1,000 terms, from Administrative Law to White Collar Crime.

part

2

Crime Connections on the Web: Criminal Justice Education in the U.S.

http://www.appstate.edu/~robinsnmb/education.htm

A professor at Appalachain State University put together this listing of undergraduate and graduate programs, arranged alphabetically.

Criminal Justice Links: Criminal Justice Education

http://www.fsu.edu/~crimdo/cjed.html

A professor at Florida State University put together this listing of graduate and undergraduate programs. It includes training institutes, continuing legal education, entry tests, and job searches.

Graduate Schools in Criminal Justice: A State-by-State Guide

http://faculty.ncwc.edu/toconnor/jusgrad.htm

A professor at North Carolina Wesleyan College put together this listing of all master's and doctoral degree programs. It includes a sample curriculum.

Phil Reichel's Criminal Justice Education Page

http://www.cjed.com/

A professor at the University of Northern Colorado put together this site to assist both criminal justice students and professors.

CRIMINAL JUSTICE EMPLOYMENT
Criminal Justice MegaLinks: Employment MegaLinks

`http://faculty.ncwc.edu/toconnor/employ.htm`

A site put together by a professor for his students and others as a guide to obtaining employment in criminal justice fields. The site offers original content as well as an extensive collection of Internet resources.

LeoLinks: Employment

`http://www.leolinks.com/employment/`

An extensive jobs page from a mega-site in policing. Résumé-posting is allowed, and there are career guides online.

www.Officer.com: Jobs

`http://www.officer.com/jobs.htm`

The jobs page from the most popular Web site in law enforcement. There are federal jobs listed and the rest of the page is organized state-by-state.

part

2

CRIMINAL JUSTICE HISTORY
The Crime Library

`http://www.crimelibrary.com/`

A site with factual and fictionalized accounts of famous criminals, serial killers, gangsters, spies, and assassins.

Criminal Justice History Resources

`http://arapaho.nsuok.edu/~dreveskr/cjhr.html-ssi`

A professor at Northeastern State University (Oklahoma) put together this amazing collection of links arranged by historical time periods.

CRIMINAL JUSTICE PROCEDURE
Anatomy of a Prosecution

`http://www.co.eaton.mi.us/ecpa/process.htm`

This is one of the best criminal justice sites on the Internet. It takes you step-by-step through all the processes, from arrest to final appeal.

APA Division 41's Psychology and Law Links

`http://www.unl.edu/ap-ls/`

A collection of psychology and law links from this group of psychologists interested in law.

Admissibility of Scientific Evidence under Daubert

`http://faculty.ncwc.edu/toconnor/daubert.htm`

An essay and informative article on what weight should be placed on various types of evidence, like fingerprinting, DNA, voice analysis, and so forth.

Criminal Defense Online

`http://www.sado.org/`

A site that explains the basics of the criminal justice system from a know-your-rights perspective. Contains samples and illustrations of various documents, such as presentence investigative reports, legal briefs, and requests for information under the Freedom of Information Act.

Effective Search and Seizure

`http://www.fsu.edu/~crimdo/fagan.html`

An online essay by a Florida State University professor which delves into the details of probable cause.

Evidence Site

`http://www.law.umich.edu/thayer/`

A site constructed by and mostly for lawyers to better understand the changes in evidence law. Contains newsletters, conference reports, recommended readings, and some suggested links.

Expert Testimony on Eyewitness Reliability

`http://www.sado.org/19cdn12.htm#19cdn12a`

An online essay that explains quite a bit about eyewitness testimony, the errors associated with it, and how experts can either bolster or destroy the testimony of an eyewitness.

FAQs about Grand Juries

`http://www.udayton.edu/~grandjur/`

This is one of the best resources on the Internet for information about juries in general and grand juries in particular.

Format of a Criminal Trial

`http://faculty.ncwc.edu/toconnor/trialfrm.htm`

This site contains a summary table and extensive, real-life descriptions of the steps in a criminal trial.

part

2

Fully Informed Jury Association

http://nowscape.com/fija/fija_us.htm

This is an excellent source of information on the Internet. The site covers issues such as jury reform, jury nullification, and the image of justice on television shows.

Handbook for Trial Jurors

http://www.ncmd.uscourts.gov/jurhbook.htm

An extensive and practical guide to everything a jury is supposed to do.

Landmark Cases in Psychiatry and Law

http://ualvm.ua.edu/~jhooper/landmark.html

This sites explores the landmark cases that added things like competency to stand trial and insanity to criminal procedure.

part

2

Legal Survival Guide

http://www.courttv.com/legalhelp/lawguide/criminal/

This is an excellent site that walks you through, step-by-step, all the stages of criminal procedure, from affidavit to appeal. The topics of pretrial procedures are covered as well as trial procedures.

Miranda Law: A Guide to the Privilege against Self-Incrimination

http://faculty.ncwc.edu/toconnor/miranda.htm

A site that provides extensive detail on the Miranda warnings that police officers should give you.

Nolo Press

http://www.nolo.com/

A publishing company's site that provides a number of online resources and self-help guides for people in trouble with the law.

Online Directory of Expert Witnesses

http://www.claims.com/

A site where different experts from around the country have deposited their resumes in hopes that someone trying a case could use their services.

Pardon Me: The Pardon Resource Center

http://www.silicon-valley.com/pardonme/index.shtml

A site that focuses exclusively on pardons, executive clemency, expungements, and so forth.

PreTrial Professionals of Florida

http://www.appf.org

A comprehensive law site focusing exclusively on pretrial procedures such as the filing of affidavits and motions in the state of Florida.

Scientific Testimony: Tutorials

http://www.scientific.org/tutorials/tutorial.html

This site, part of an online journal, contains articles on DNA testing and DNA exonerations which are written in laymen's terms.

Search and Seizure: A Guide to Rules, Requirements, Tests, Doctrines, and Special Circumstances

http://faculty.ncwc.edu/toconnor/serchrul.htm

A site that provides extensive detail on searches and seizures by the police.

TnCrimLaw

http://www.tncrimlaw.com/

Part of Carpenter's site in forensic science, TnCrimLaw on this page has a section called Explanations in Everyday Language which contains concise explanations of key criminal justice procedures, like What is an Arraignment? What is a Preliminary Hearing? What is a Grand Jury? There's even an online glossary of terms in criminal justice.

CRIMINAL JUSTICE REFORM

Children's Defense Fund

http://www.childrensdefense.org/

An influential lobby group devoted to being the voice for all children in America. Their Web site contains information about the stands they take on important issues affecting children's rights, such as those involving being a victim of crime.

part

2

Citizens United for the Rehabilitation of Errants

http://www.curenational.org/index.html

CURE is an advocacy and lobby organization for the reduction of crime through criminal law reform. It opposes capital punishment and control units, favoring instead more use of education and programs. Their Web site offers original and Internet resources.

Criminal Justice MegaLinks: A Glossary of Social Reforms

http://faculty.ncwc.edu/toconnor/reform.htm

An online, hyperlinked encyclopedia with listings from A to Z on every social experiment or feat of social engineering tried in the late twentieth century to fight crime, fight poverty, and improve society.

Families against Mandatory Minimums

http://www.famm.org/

This nonprofit organization, which claims that the criminal justice system is broken, proposes and documents extensively the reasons why mandatory minimum sentences should be abolished. The site offers original and Internet resources on sentencing reform.

Freedom Forum

http://www.freedomforum.org/

This is a First Amendment watchdog group with information on their site about free speech, press, religion, and assembly.

Howard League for Penal Reform

http://web.ukonline.co.uk/howard.league/

Based in the United Kingdom, this charity organization, founded by John Howard, has historical importance. Their site offers a number of original publications and has an extensive collection of Internet resource links on many different aspects of penal reform.

Injustice Line

http://home.earthlink.net/~ynot/

A Web site dedicated to exposing and publicizing injustices. One of the features at this site is a list of twelve justice system reforms.

part

2

Justice for All

`http://www.jfa.net/`

A victims-oriented reform group with a pro-death penalty stance.

Koch Crime Institute

`http://www.kci.org/`

A nonprofit organization that studies the criminal and juvenile justice system in an effort to reduce crime, especially juvenile crime. Their site has a juvenile boot camp directory, a collection of links on methamphetamine use, and resources on the privatization of prisons.

National Urban League

`http://www.nul.org`

A group to assist African Americans in the achievement of social and economic equality.

Paul's Justice Page

`http://www.paulsjusticepage.com/stopviolence/index.htm`

A site put together by students at Eastern Michigan University on school violence, hate crime, and violence prevention.

part

2

Peacemaking and Crime

`http://www.westga.edu/~jfuller/peace.html`

Professor John Fuller's site at University of West Georgia is an excellent resource on various alternative justice systems.

Prison Activist Resource Center

`http://www.prisonactivist.org/`

The extensive site has a number of resources on prison reform.

RAND

`http://www.rand.org/`

A public policy think tank with online resources in criminal justice policy analysis, drugs and crime, immigration and crime, sentencing, drug control, and violence reduction. The site contains copies of recent publications and newsletters.

Redwood Highway: System Critique and Reform

`http://www.sonoma.edu/cja/info/infop6.html`

Part of a mega-site with essays and links on alternative and progressive thoughts about the criminal justice system.

Sentencing Project

`http://www.sentencingproject.org/`

The Sentencing Project is an independent source of policy analysis and information for the public about sentencing. They support the Campaign for an Effective Crime Policy, and their site has extensive resources on school violence, boot camps, drug courts, mandatory minimums, and the relationship between imprisonment and the crime rate.

Stop Prisoner Rape

`http://www.igc.org/spr/`

A nonprofit organization with their Web site hosted on IGC that takes an activist stance toward ending the prison and jailhouse rapes of prisoners. They provide extensive news coverage and other features on their site.

True Justice to the Unjust

`http://members.tripod.com/~MerlM/index.html`

An angry kind of site that is posting every known instance in the news about crimes by the police, judicial misconduct, and correctional abuses.

Vera Institute of Justice

`http://www.vera.org/`

A nonprofit think tank that is devoted to finding creative and innovative alternatives to punishment like imprisonment. The Vera Institute has conducted research on jury reform and appearance in court, two areas where they make their studies public on their Web site. The Vera Institute Web site also has an excellent collection of justice-related Internet resources.

CRIMINOLOGY

Australian Institute of Criminology

`http://www.aic.gov.au/`

An extensive site that reviews the worldwide criminological literature for possible policy applications in Australia and elsewhere.

Crime Magazine

http://www.crimemagazine.com/

An online publishing venue which covers mostly celebrity crime, serial crime, sex crime, and organized crime.

CrimeTheory.com

http://www.crimetheory.com/

A site created by Prof. Bruce Hoffman at the University of Washington which contains extensive resources on criminological theories and theorists.

Crime Times

http://www.crime-times.org/

An online newsletter and other resources specifically devoted to biological theories and research into the causes of criminal behavior.

Criminal Justice MegaLinks: Criminology

http://faculty.ncwc.edu/toconnor/criminology.htm

An academic site put together by a professor to explain criminological theory, motives for crime underlying the theories, and policy implications.

Criminal Psychology

http://www.geocities.com/CapitolHill/Lobby/6027/

This site contains serious and amusing resources on the psychological causes of criminal behavior.

Criminological Theory

http://personal.tmlp.com/ddemelo/crime/
crimetheory.html

This is a site which was created by Professor Diane DeMelo which outlines the major theories in criminology, some of which have active links which lead to a fuller explanation of the theory.

Critical Criminology Division Home Page

http://sun.soci.niu.edu/~critcrim/

An academic site with extensive resources on restorative justice, peacemaking criminology, the death penalty, gun control, wrongful conviction, and more.

part
2

DSM Criteria

http://www.apa.org/science/lib.html

An APA site that consists of the terms and definitions of DSM criteria, focusing specifically upon such concepts of abnormal behavior like psychopath and sociopath.

Measuring, Explaining, and Confronting Crime

http://local.uaa.alaska.edu/~afdsw/crime.html

A professor at the University of Alaska put this site together to explain how crime is measured, explained, and confronted using various Internet resources as hyperlinks in the sentences.

Rational Criminals and Intentional Accidents

http://www.best.com/~ddfr/Academic/Hidden_Order/
Hidden_Order_Chapter_20.html

An economic point of view on law breaking.

Sociological Theories of Deviance

http://www.d.umn.edu/~jhamlin1/soc3305.html

This is a site created by Professor John Hamlin at the University of Minnesota which provides notes on various sociological explanations for crime.

Sociological Tour through HyperSpace: Theories

http://www.trinity.edu/~mkearl/theory.html

An excellent collection of Internet resource links on sociological theories.

SocioRealm: Criminology

http://www.geocities.com/CollegePark/Quad/5889/

This excellent and resourceful site has a section on criminology which includes links to all sorts of papers and articles on criminological theory, adult and juvenile violence, corporate crime, and criminal justice links.

Solon's Voyage

http://www.geocities.com/Athens/Acropolis/7001/

This site, located in Australia, is an excellent resource for everything about women and law, women and criminology, and sentencing from a woman's perspective.

Vault of Sociology

`http://www.sla.purdue.edu/people/soc/mdeflem/`
`work8vau.html`

A rather humorous site about sociological and criminological theory.

Western Society of Criminology

`http://www.sonoma.edu/cja/wsc/wscmain.html`

Actually two sites in one, this URL provides you with online newsletter and journal articles about crime and criminological theory.

DEATH PENALTY
Anti-Death Penalty Resources

`http://sun.soci.niu.edu/~critcrim/dp/dp.html`

An excellent resource site from the ASC Division of Critical Criminology. Includes statistics from recent years, fact sheets, Supreme Court decisions, and generalized and specific links.

part
2

Death Penalty Information Center

`http://www.deathpenaltyinfo.org/`

A fact-filled site useful for research on race, women, juveniles, the mentally retarded, and capital punishment.

Death Penalty Links

`http://www.derechos.org/dp/`

A lengthy collection of links and original essays from the Derechos Human Rights Campaign.

Death Penalty News

`http://www.smu.edu/~deathpen/`

An online newsletter that tracks scheduled executions by name and state. Other Internet resource links are provided.

Death, Reason, and Judgment: The American Experience

`http://lgxserver.uniba.it/lei/filpol/allen.htm`

An interesting commentary that argues against getting tough on crime from a financial or economic point of view.

ElectricChair.com

http://www.theelectricchair.com/

A rather shocking site that focuses upon the history of electrocution and answers almost every question imaginable about it.

Fatal Flaws: Innocence and the Death Penalty

http://www.amnesty.org/ailib/aipub/1998/AMR/
25106998.htm

A lengthy 1998 article from Amnesty International, significant for its superb investigative research on inmates who were executed but later found innocent.

Professor David's Death Penalty Resources

http://www.uncp.edu/home/vanderhoof/death.html

A professor put this site together to stimulate critical thinking about the death penalty. It organizes Internet resources in an interesting way.

Punishment and the Death Penalty

http://ethics.acusd.edu/death_penalty.html

This site contains discussion and links about punishment in general and the death penalty in particular.

DRUGS

National Clearinghouse for Drug and Alcohol Information

http://www.health.org

Resources and online data on federal, state, and local anti-drug initiatives. A good starting place for drug researchers.

National Drug Prevention League

http://www.ndpl.org/

An association of private sector organizations for drug abuse prevention. The site provides links to Internet resources and information, including national surveys and studies, federal programs, and proposed legislation.

National Institute of Alcohol Abuse and Alcoholism

http://www.niaaa.nih.gov/

A division of the National Institute of Health which was constructed to combat alcohol problems by providing reports about them.

National Institute of Drug Abuse

http://www.nida.nih.gov

A division of the National Institute of Health which contains much of the research that is known about drug abuse and addiction.

Partnership for a Drug-Free America

http://www.drugfreeamerica.org/

This site has a comprehensive database of drug information, what to do, what drugs look like, their history, and slang terms.

Policing for Profit: The Drug War's Hidden Economic Agenda

http://www.fear.org/chicago.html

A rather lengthy, but important, paper on the policies of asset forfeiture and using R.I.C.O. statutes to confiscate the defendant's property.

Reddy's Forensic Links: Drugs

http://haven.ios.com/~nyrc/new15.htm

Part of a mega-site in forensic science that focuses upon drugs, drug interactions, and what the experts say in terms of how it influences criminal behavior.

part 2

Ultimate Drug Links Resource

http://www.algonet.se/~birdy/druglink/

An alphabetical listing of every drug known throughout history.

Web of Addictions

http://www.well.com/user/woa/

A site dedicated to providing accurate information about alcohol and other drugs as a resource for teachers, students, and others who need factual information about abused drugs and addictive behavior.

GANGS AND JUVENILE CRIME

American Bar Associations Juvenile Justice Center

http://www.abanet.org/crimjust/juvjus/home.html

A special feature Web site with online publications, articles, and links on juvenile justice and the special due process safeguards therein.

Florida State's Juvenile Justice Clearinghouse

```
http://www.fsu.edu/~crimdo/jjclearinghouse/
jjclearinghouse.html
```

One of Florida State's research centers, the site explains what research they carry out, and what policy recommendations they have made.

Greg's Gang Page

```
http://members.aol.com/ggarner539/index.html
```

This site has an extensive collection of links, photos, and book reviews. The gangs covered are Midwest gangs, Asian gangs, and biker gangs.

A Guide to Gangs

```
http://www.dc.state.fl.us/pub/gangs/index.html
```

A site provided by the Florida Department of Corrections that is about prison gangs in Florida and elsewhere. It provides extensive information about the history, symbols, and identifiers for at least six major gangs, including Chicago-based and L.A.-based ones. There's also a guide to basic facts about gangs and answers to frequently asked questions.

Juvenile Boot Camp Directory

```
http://www.kci.org/publication/bootcamp/
prerelease.htm
```

A page from the Koch Crime Institute site which shows a map of the nation's juvenile boot camps. There are additional links on the page from government publications on boot camps.

Juvenile Justice Home Page

```
http://www.edwardhumes.com/links.htm#juvenile
```

This site provides excellent resources on the history of the juvenile court and links to contemporary research reports.

LeoLinks: Gang Links

```
http://www.leolinks.com/search/
Intelligence__Crime_Stats/Gangs/index.shtml
```

A long list of gang links of interest to police officers.

part

2

Midwest Gang Investigators Association

http://members.aol.com/GGarner539/index.html

An AOL home page created by a correctional officer which offers extensive resources on gang definitions, gang activities, guides to Midwest gangs, recommended readings, and links to other state gang investigation sites.

National Youth Gang Center

http://www.iir.com/nygc/

This Center assists state and local governments in the collection, analysis, and exchange of information on gang-related demographics, legislation, literature, research, and promising strategies. It is an excellent resource for gang researchers.

NCJRS Index of Juvenile Justice Documents

http://www.ncjrs.org/jjhome.htm

Online documents from this government information clearinghouse.

SocioRealm: Gang Violence

http://www.geocities.com/CollegePark/Quad/5889/

This informative and useful site has an excellent collection of links on the topic of gang violence, its explanation, and its control.

Street Gang Dynamics

http://www.gangwar.com/dynamics.htm

A free, online book from gangwar.com that is worth reading in its entirety as a beginner's manual on understanding street gangs, their motivations, and graffiti interpretation.

HUMAN RIGHTS
American Civil Liberties Union

http://www.aclu.org/

An organizational lobby site that serves as a legal defense resource for various civil rights groups, including immigrants, gays and lesbians, minorities, and victims of discrimination. It has extensive resources on free speech, cyberliberties, and criminal justice issues.

part
2

Amnesty International

http://www.amnesty.org/

An international watchdog group that documents criminal justice system incidents of torture, brutality, and violations of human rights.

Directory of Human Rights Resources on the Internet

http://shr.aaas.org/dhr.htm

A huge collection of human rights-related resources, indexed topically and geographically.

Human Rights Watch Prison Project

http://www.hrw.org/advocacy/prisons/index.htm

Part of the Human Rights Web (http://www.hrweb.org/), this site is dedicated to ending the abusive treatment of prisoners. Human Rights Watch has conducted specialized prison research and helped to focus international attention on prison conditions worldwide. Their site details the most common abuses inflicted on prisoners.

IGC Network

http://www.igc.org/igc/

The largest political activist site on the Internet that includes extensive resources on women and crime, race and crime, and social justice.

National Civil Rights Museum

http://www.midsouth.rr.com/civilrights/

A multimedia tour of the civil rights movement.

LAW

Constitution Notebook Program

http://members.aol.com/tcnbp/

The owner of this site wants to sell his Constitutional Law guide to you, but most of his site is freely accessible. This sites makes for an excellent Constitutional Law source. Almost every line in the Constitution is analyzed word-for-word.

Constitutional Law: An Overview

http://www.law.cornell.edu/topics/constitutional.html

The simplest and most concise summary of the whole field of Constitutional Law on the Internet, from Cornell's Legal Information Institute.

Criminal Justice Links: Searchable Law Databases

http://www.fsu.edu/~crimdo/law.html

This page has an extensive listing of law links, but its main feature is its annotated listing of the various legal research search engines.

Criminal Justice MegaLinks: Mega-Guide to Law and Law Schools

http://faculty.ncwc.edu/toconnor/megalaw.htm

This page provides links and essays on different types of law, what it's like to study the law, and has a comprehensive list of all Law Schools in the United States with their entry requirements.

Criminal Law Links

http://dpa.state.ky.us/~rwheeler/

This site, put together by the Kentucky Department of Public Advocacy, has an extensive collection of law links, especially in the area of correctional law. The site also contains an online newsletter and other original resources.

part

2

Duhaime's Legal Dictionary

http://www.wwlia.org/diction.htm

An online legal dictionary, written free of charge, by a lawyer.

FindLaw

http://www.findlaw.com/

An easy-to-use legal search engine with topical guides.

Five Hour Law School

http://members.aol.com/ronin48th/hope.htm

A site that explains in five hours everything that a lawyer is trained in and what lawyers do. There's an online glossary of terms, but the best feature is the explanation of which of those books in the library to use first.

Hieros Gamos: The Comprehensive Law Site

http://www.hg.org/

A large site covering many different areas of law from all over the world.

Law Guru

http://www.lawguru.com/

An "ask-the-expert" site with previously posted questions and answers.

Law and Politics Internet Guide

http://www.geocities.com/CapitolHill/Lobby/5011/

A site designed for one-stop shopping in your legal research needs. You can use the topical guides to things like death penalty resources, or there's an extremely flexible search engine.

Law School Admissions Council

http://www.lsac.org/

This is the site for the organization that administers the LSAT entry exam for law schools. It has extensive resources, including sample exams and financial aid help pages.

part
2

Legal Information Institute

http://www.law.cornell.edu/

This site at Cornell University is widely regarded as the best site on the Internet for law. There are topical guides to the law in common areas like the Constitution, Criminal Law, and Criminal Procedure. All of the U.S. Codes as well as all recent and historical Supreme Court cases are online and searchable by number or by name. Opinions of the Appeals courts are also online.

Legal Research Online

http://www.galaxy.com/galaxy/Government/Law.html

There's an assortment of resources at this site, featuring mostly examples of different forms used in the practice of law.

Quid Pro Quo

http://members.tripod.com/~quidproquo/titlepage.html

A law student help site with links to online lectures, a jobs board, humorous tests to see if you're law school material, and much more.

State Laws on the Internet

http://www.megalaw.com/

This site provides links to every state at which the criminal law can be looked up, commentary and comparisons can be found, and legal research can almost be conducted.

WashLaw Web: Washburn University School of Law

http://www.washlaw.edu/

An extensive and well-organized set of state law links.

Web Guide to the Constitution

http://members.aol.com/tcnbp/USCons1.htm

A short, but complete, section-by-section and amendment-by-amendment analysis of the Constitution.

POLICE

911 Theory and Operations

http://www.hotcity.com/911/

An excellent site that explains everything you would want to know about 911 emergency services.

Broken Windows

http://www.theatlantic.com/unbound/flashbks/crime/crime.htm

The web reposting of an early, influential article called "Broken Windows," written by James Q. Wilson and George Kelling at this *Atlantic Monthly* Flashbacks site.

part

2

Carolina's Institute for Community Policing

http://www.cicp.org/

A research center and institute with numerous reports and essays online about the more high-tech end of community policing.

Community Policing Consortium

http://www.communitypolicing.org/

A site with online lectures and other training materials to learn about the many aspects of community policing.

Community Policing Pages

http://www.concentric.net/~dwoods/tribute.htm

A tribute site to the founder of community policing, Robert Trojanowicz. The site also contains horror stories of community policing gone wrong.

CopLink

http://www.coplink.com/copops.htm

This is a site about the basic functions of law enforcement, such as patrol work, traffic safety, and detective work.

Exposing Police Racism

http://www.bwbadge.com/

A site dedicated to exposing and combatting police racism and corruption.

Fighting Police Abuse

http://www.aclu.org/library/
fighting_police_abuse.html

An extensive Web site put together by the ACLU to expose and combat police brutality and police spying.

part
2

History of the Berkeley Police Department

http://209.232.44.30/bpd_history/history.htm

A site that details the history of this department and its influential police chief and famous police reformer, August Vollmer.

History of the Metropolitan Police Service

http://www.met.police.uk/police/mps/mps/history/
mishist0.htm

A site that chronicles the origin of the London "Bobbies" and their founder, Sir Robert Peel.

History of the Pennsylvania State Police

http://www.state.pa.us/PA_Exec/State_Police/
history/history.htm

A site about what history regards as the first professional state police.

Law Enforcement Links on the Web

http://www.ih2000.net/ira/ira.htm

A mega-site with thousands of police links, arranged on big pages.

Law Enforcement Online

`http://www.pimacc.pima.edu/dps/police.htm`

This is an excellent and fairly complete collection of law enforcement agencies with Web sites.

LawSearch: The Police Officer's Search Engine

`http://www.copscgi.com/`

This site has an extremely well-organized database and site layout. You can search for topics such as police humor or technology. There are sections of the site for downloading shareware and for entering a chat room.

LeoLinks

`http://www.leolinks.com/`

One of the largest sites in policing, LeoLinks categorizes resources by type of police operation, type of agency, and type of crime. There is an extensive array of other resources, including mailing lists and discussion forums.

part

2

Miami Metro-Dade Police Department

`http://www.mdpd.com`

An example of a consolidated, city-county police department.

Nassau County (NY) Police Department

`http://www.co.nassau.ny.us/police/index.html`

One of the nation's largest county police departments.

National Trooper's Coalition

`http://www.sover.net/~tmartin/State.htm`

A directory of all state police departments in the United States.

New Blue Line

`http://www.pilotonline.com/special/blueline/`

This site is about how police work changes your personality, affects your health, and indoctrinates you into a police subculture you can't get out of.

New York City Police Department

`http://www.ci.nyc.ny.us/html/nypd/home.html`

The largest municipal police department in the United States.

Organization of the Royal Canadian Mounted Police

http://www.rcmp-grc.gc.ca/html/organiz.htm

An excellent Web site with tons of information about the RCMP.

PIMA's List of Military Police Departments Online

http://www.pima.edu/dps/Mil.htm

A collection of military police Web sites.

Police Guide

http://www.policeguide.com/

A large site in policing which tends to be focused on collectibles, but there are other interesting online resources in the way of memorabilia and a good guide to cop culture.

Police and Policing

http://local.uaa.alaska.edu/~afdsw/police.html

An online, hyperlink essay about policing from this University of Alaska professor's site.

Police Brutality and Excessive Force

http://www.amnesty.it/AIlibtop/1996/AMR/25103696.htm

A report from Amnesty International on the New York City police department.

Police Officer Stress and Agency Structure

http://www.ifip.com/acjs1rr.htm

An interesting article about the inherent stresses of police work.

Police Stress Line

http://www.geocities.com/~halbrown/index4.html

A site containing original articles and other content dealing exclusively with various topics in the area of police stress. The author of this Web site is a police stress therapist.

Police Structure of the United States

http://faculty.ncwc.edu/toconnor/polstruct.htm

An online essay and directory of links for federal, state, county, and municipal police departments.

part

2

Small Town and Rural Crime Page

http://www.ilstu.edu/depts/cjs/rural.htm

An online bibliography and collection of essays about small town policing and how it's different from big city policing.

Status of Women in Policing

http://www.feminist.org/police/ncwp.html

A comprehensive site reporting the status of women in policing and containing several other essays or sources of information on issues related to women and policing, including the police family.

Texas Ranger's Hall of Fame and Museum

http://www.texasranger.org/

A site that tells the history of the first state police force.

www.Officer.com

http://www.officer.com/

The largest directory of police departments and their special units on the Internet.

REHABILITATION

Drama Therapy in Criminal Justice

http://members.aol.com/MacFlap/Geesetheatre.html

This site claims that by using psychodrama and other performing art techniques, many criminal offenders can be rehabilitated.

Institute of Behavioral Research

http://www.ibr.tcu.edu/projects/crimjust/pta.html

An Institute at Texas Christian University which is dedicated full-time to the study of substance abuse treatment issues in prison. Their site has project reports, recidivism studies, and a newsletter.

National Institute for the Psychotherapies

http://www.nipinst.org/

A group that conducts training programs to enhance the development of mental health treatment skills.

PsychWeb

http://www.psychwww.com/

An exhaustive site on all aspects of psychology and particularly strong in the area of abnormal psychology.

Psychology Information Online

http://www.psychologyinfo.com/

An extensive site with excellent resources in forensic psychology and applications of psychology to diagnosis and treatment of problems relating to criminal behavior or being a victim of crime.

Reducing Recidivism: What Works?

http://www.bestweb.net/~cureny/

Online articles that contain scholarly reviews of the research summarizing much of what we know about rehabilitating prisoners.

part 2

Treatment of Violent Offenders

http://www.csc-scc.gc.ca/text/publicsubject_e.shtml

Online research reports by the Canadian government that review the current literature about what works and what doesn't in the treatment or rehabilitation of criminal offenders.

Yahoo Guide to Corrections and Rehabilitation

http://dir.yahoo.com/society_and_culture/crime/
correction_and_rehabilitation/

A site with listings by topics including prison survival guides, pen pals, correctional education services, and many other issues.

VIOLENT AND SERIAL CRIME
Armed Robbery Page

http://www.ior.com/~jdmoore/

A site devoted to the topic of holdups, resistance issues, and employee training at financial institutions.

Assault Prevention Information Network

http://www.nsm.smcm.edu/Chemistry/Darlene/
VAWPIN-home.htm

A site that contains information about self-defense resources, martial arts resources, violence in society, and violence prevention.

Bad Men Do What Good Men Dream

http://www.appi.org/simonb.html

An online essay by a forensic psychologist on sexual serial killers.

Child Abuse Prevention Network

http://child.cornell.edu/

A site providing an almost inexhaustible collection of links on anything to do with child abuse.

Communities against Violence Network

http://www.cavnet.org/

Communities against Violence, or CAVNET, is a good resource site on violence against women, minorities, gays/lesbians, people with disabilities, the crime of stalking, and more.

Domestic Violence Handbook

http://www.domesticviolence.org/

An online resource designed to assist women who are experiencing domestic abuse.

Genesis of a Serial Killer

http://www.jurai.net/~patowic/genesis.html

An online essay about the role of fantasy, addiction, and compulsion in the way some people are brought up which turns them into serial killers, according to this article at least.

Homicide Research Working Group

http://www.icpsr.umich.edu/NACJD/HRWG/

An academic association that publishes the journal, *Homicide Studies*. Only earlier transcripts of their workshops are available online.

Internet Crime Archives

http://www.mayhem.net/Crime/archives.html

A rather shocking site on serial killers, cult killers, and mass murderers.

Justice for All

http://www.jfa.net

A citizens reform group with an excellent collection of links on stalking, gun violence, pro-death penalty resources, and victim's rights.

part

2

Men and Women against Domestic Violence

http://www.silcom.com/~paladin/madv/

An informative site with statistics, answers to frequently asked questions, and links to Internet resources on violence against women, including rape.

Minnesota Center against Violence and Abuse

http://www.mincava.umn.edu/

This site has an extensive listing of resources on all kinds of violence against children, women, minorities, and the elderly. It also includes links on gun, school, television, workplace, and gang violence.

National Gay and Lesbian Task Force

http://www.ngltf.org

A site with extensive information on gay-bashing and other hate crimes against sexual minorities.

Partnerships against Violence Network

http://www.pavnet.org/

Partnerships against Violence, or PAVNET, acts as a virtual library or clearinghouse to prevent redundant information on topics related to violence and youth-at-risk.

Serial Killer Information Site

http://www.serialkillers.net/

Information in the form of serial killer case studies, including links to sites on forensics and criminal profiling.

Sexual Assault Information Page

http://www.cs.utk.edu/~bartley/saInfoPage.html

Academic Internet resources alphabetized by type of rape: acquaintance rape, date rape, serial rape, etc.

WHITE COLLAR, ORGANIZED, AND PROPERTY CRIME

Committee for a Safe Society: Organized Crime Menu

http://www.alternatives.com/crime/menu.html

Extensive resource site for links on organized crime groups by country of origin, the international slavery trade, money laundering, and crimes against the environment.

Consumer Law Page

`http://www.consumerlawpage.com/`

This site has resources on negligence, injury, toxins, and corporate crime.

Cybrary: Burglary

`http://talkjustice.com/files/page51.htm`

A collection of Internet resources on burglary techniques and prevention.

Financial Scandals

`http://www.ex.ac.uk/~RDavies/arian/scandals/`

An excellent resource site on bank scams, political corruption, and organized crime.

Fire and Arson Investigation Resource Page

`http://home.earthlink.net/~dliske/`

A useful site with links, a dictionary, and articles on what motivates arsonists and firestarters.

HateWatch

`http://hatewatch.org/frames.html`

An extensive resource site with listings of hate groups, church bombings, and bigotry on the Internet.

International Policy Institute for Counter-Terrorism

`http://www.ict.org.il/`

A think tank's Web site with many online articles and the latest news.

MIT Guide to Lockpicking

`http://www.lysator.liu.se/mit-guide/mit-guide.html`

The definitive guide on how people break into things.

**part
2**

National Check Fraud Center

http://www.ckfraud.org/

An intelligence collection site on the most common types of financial crimes, including forgery, scams, counterfeiting, and fraud.

Organized Crime Registry

http://members.tripod.com/~orgcrime/index.htm

Coverage of drug cartels and other crime syndicates.

Southern Poverty Law Center

http://www.splcenter.org/

Home of KlanWatch and other militia group monitoring activities.

Web of Justice: Organized Crime Links

http://www.co.pinellas.fl.us/bcc/juscoord/
eorganized.htm

An extensive collection of organized crime links available on the Internet, covers Al Capone to the Yakuza and includes special police units.

E-Journals, Magazines, and Newsletters

APA Journals

http://www.apa.org/journals/

A listing of all journals published by the American Psychological Association.

Criminal Justice Links: Online Journals and Listservs

http://www.fsu.edu/~crimdo/listserv.html

A mega-list of online journals and discussion lists in criminal justice.

Criminal Justice Policy Review

http://www.iup.edu/cr/CJPR/

Only abstracts available online from this journal.

Ethics and Justice

`http://www.ethics-justice.org/`

Journal for ethics in criminology and criminal Justice with some online articles.

FBI Law Enforcement Bulletin

`http://www.fbi.gov/library/leb/leb.htm`

This is the online version of a monthly journal by the FBI.

Injustice Studies

`http://wolf.its.ilstu.edu/injustice/`

Online journal about worldwide atrocities.

International Journal of Drug Testing

`http://www.criminology.fsu.edu/journal/`

An online journal of research on forensic techniques to detect drugs.

Journal of Credibility Assessment and Witness Psychology

`http://truth.boisestate.edu/jcaawp/default.html`

An online journal about issues in forensic science and testimony.

Journal of Criminal Justice Ethics

`http://www.lib.jjay.cuny.edu/cje/`

An online journal site with a collection of links that are labeled as the most useful links in the field. Some of the journal articles are viewable.

Journal of Criminal Justice and Popular Culture

`http://www.albany.edu/scj/jcjpc/`

An online journal that reviews crime images in the media.

Journal of Online Law

`http://www.wm.edu/law/publications/jol/`

Online journal devoted to emerging cyberspace law issues.

part

2

Journal of Prisoners on Prisoners

http://www.jpp.org/

A rather unique online journal written by prisoners about prisoners.

The Keeper's Voice

http://www.oicj.org/public/

Online newsletter of the International Association of Correctional Officers.

Law and Order Magazine

http://www.lawandordermag.com/

Browsing permitted at this law enforcement magazine site.

Links to Psychological and Social Science Journals

http://www.psywww.com/resource/journals.htm

An index of more than 1,000 links to psychology and social science journal sites.

part

2

Online Social Science Journals

http://hypatia.ss.uci.edu/democ/journal.htm

A mega-list of online social science journals, mostly in politics, some in sociology.

Redwood Highway: Electronic Journals

http://www.sonoma.edu/cja/info/infop8.html

A mega-list of electronic journals in criminal justice.

Security Management

http://www.securitymanagement.com/

Online magazine for private security professionals.

Science and Justice

http://www.demon.co.uk/forensic/jnltop.html

Online journal of the Forensic Science Society.

Scientific Testimony

`http://www.scientific.org/`

An online journal in forensic science.

Theoretical Criminology

`http://www.sagepub.co.uk/journals/details/j0064.html`

Some abstracts are available online for this journal.

Western Criminology Review

`http://wcr.sonoma.edu/`

An excellent online journal with articles on types of crime and justice.

Listservs and Mailing Lists

- CJUST-L: Except for POLICE-L, which is a closed list, this is the world's largest discussion list dedicated to justice issues, where anything goes, except discussion of the right to bear arms. It's hosted by City University of New York's, John Jay College. For information on joining, visit their Web site at **http://listserv.cuny.edu/archives/ cjust-l.html.**

- Crime and Clues-L: An open forum for people interested in crime scenes and criminal investigation. For information on joining, visit their Web site at **http://www.dejanews.com/~crimeandclues.**

- CRIT-L: This is the discussion list of the Critical Criminology Division of the American Society of Criminology. It's open to anyone supporting the goals of the division. There's lots of discussion of topical criminal justice issues like the death penalty. For information on joining, visit their Web site at **http://sun.soci.niu.edu/~archives/ CRIT-L/crit-l.html.**

- LEANALYST-L: A discussion list for law enforcement analysts, but open to students and anyone interested in analyzing crime. For information on joining, visit their Web site at **http:// www.inteltec.com/leanalyst/.**

- NICPUBLIC-L: Official discussion list for the National Institute of Corrections, but open to the public. For information on joining, visit their Web site at **http://www.nicic.org/lists.htm.**

part

2

- PRISON-L: This is a discussion list on prison issues and various prison topics hosted by Yale University. To subscribe, send email to listproc@lists.yale.edu with nothing in the subject box and only the words subscribe PRISON-L FirstName LastName in the body of your message.

- Prisons-L: A mailing list for the discussion of issues of concern to correctional officers. For information on joining, visit their Web site at **http://www.onelist.com/subscribe/Prisons.**

- Profiling-L: An open forum for anyone who has an interest in discussing methods and practices of Criminal Profiling. For information on joining, visit their Web site at **http://www.corpus-delicti.com.**

- Rule of Law-L: An open list for people interested in world crime events and the latest justice news from around the world. For information on joining, visit their Web site at **http://www.wjin.net.**

- Treatment Issues in Corrections-L: Run by a correctional employee and open to anybody. For information on joining, visit their Web site at **http://users.downcity.net/~jmm/prison.htm.**

part

2

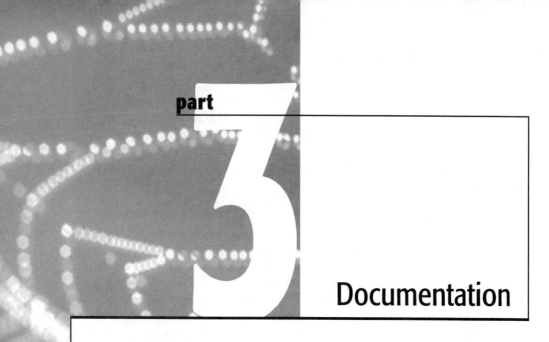

Documentation

Your Citation for Exemplary Research

There's another detail left for us to handle—the formal citing of electronic sources in academic papers. The very factor that makes research on the Internet exciting is the same factor that makes referencing these sources challenging: their dynamic nature. A journal article exists, either in print or on microfilm, virtually forever. A document on the Internet can come, go, and change without warning. Because the purpose of citing sources is to allow another scholar to retrace your argument, a good citation allows a reader to obtain information from your primary sources, to the extent possible. This means you need to include not only information on when a source was posted on the Internet (if available) but also when you obtained the information.

The two arbiters of form for academic and scholarly writing are the Modern Language Association (MLA) and the American Psychological Association (APA); both organizations have established styles for citing electronic publications.

MLA Style

In the fifth edition of the *MLA Handbook for Writers of Research Papers*, the MLA recommends the following formats:

- **URLs:** URLs are enclosed in angle brackets (<>) and contain the access mode identifier, the formal name for such indicators as "http" or "ftp." If a URL must be split across two lines, break it only after a slash (/). Never introduce a hyphen at the end of the first line. The URL should include all the parts necessary to identify uniquely the file/document being cited.

  `<http://www.csun.edu/~rtvfdept/home/index.html>`

- **An online scholarly project or reference database:** A complete online reference contains the title of the project or database (underlined); the name of the editor of the project or database (if given); electronic publication information, including version number (if relevant and if not part of the title), date of electronic publication or latest update, and name of any sponsoring institution or organization; date of access; and electronic address.

`The Perseus Project`. Ed. Gregory R. Crane. Mar. 1997.
`    Department of Classics, Tufts University. 15 June`
`    1998 <http://www.perseus.tufts.edu/>.`

If you cannot find some of the information, then include the information that is available. The MLA also recommends that you print or download electronic documents, freezing them in time for future reference.

- **A document within a scholarly project or reference database:** It is much more common to use only a portion of a scholarly project or database. To cite an essay, poem, or other short work, begin this citation with the name of the author and the title of the work (in quotation marks). Then, include all the information used when citing a complete online scholarly project or reference database, however, make sure you use the URL of the specific work and not the address of the general site.

Cuthberg, Lori. "Moonwalk: Earthlings' Finest
`    Hour."` `Discovery Channel Online`. 1999. Discovery
`    Channel. 25 Nov. 1999 <http://www.discovery.com/`
`    indep/newsfeatures/moonwa lk/challenge.html>.`

- **A professional or personal site:** Include the name of the person creating the site (reversed), followed by a period, the title of the site (underlined), or, if there is no title, a description such as Home page (such a description is neither placed in quotes nor underlined). Then, specify the name of any school, organization, or other institution affiliated with the site and follow it with your date of access and the URL of the page.

```
Packer, Andy. Home page. 1 Apr. 1998 <http://
    www.suu.edu/~students/Packer.htm>.
```

Some electronic references are truly unique to the online domain. These include email, newsgroup postings, MUDs (multiuser domains) or MOOs (multiuser domains, object-oriented), and IRCs (Internet Relay Chats).

Email   In citing email messages, begin with the writer's name (reversed) followed by a period, then the title of the message (if any) in quotations as it appears in the subject line. Next comes a description of the message, typically "Email to," and the recipient (e.g., "the author"), and finally the date of the message.

```
Davis, Jeffrey. "Web Writing Resources." Email to
    Nora Davis. 3 Jan. 2000.

Sommers, Laurice. "Re: College Admissions Practices."
    Email to the author. 12 Aug. 1998.
```

List Servers and Newsgroups   In citing these references, begin with the author's name (reversed) followed by a period. Next include the title of the document (in quotes) from the subject line, followed by the words "Online posting" (not in quotes). Follow this with the date of posting. For list servers, include the date of access, the name of the list (if known), and the online address of the list's moderator or administrator. For newsgroups, follow "Online posting" with the date of posting, the date of access, and the name of the newsgroup, prefixed with "news:" and enclosed in angle brackets.

```
Applebaum, Dale. "Educational Variables." Online
    posting. 29 Jan. 1998. Higher Education
    Discussion Group. 30 Jan. 1993
    <jlucidoj@unc.edu>.

Gostl, Jack. "Re: Mr. Levitan." Online posting.
    13 June 1997. 20 June 1997
    <news:alt.edu.bronxscience>.
```

part

3

MUDs, MOOs, and IRCs Begin with the name of the speaker(s) followed by a period. Follow with the description and date of the event, the forum in which the communication took place, the date of access, and the online address. If you accessed the MOO or MUD through telnet, your citation might appear as follows:

```
Guest. Personal interview. 13 Aug. 1998. <telnet://
     du.edu:8888>.
```

For more information on MLA documentation style for online sources, check out their Web site at http://www.mla.org/style/sources.htm.

APA Style

The *Publication Manual of the American Psychological Association* (4th ed.) is fairly dated in its handling of online sources, having been published before the rise of the WWW and the generally recognized format for URLs. The format that follows is based on the APA manual, with modifications. It's important to remember that, unlike the MLA, the APA does not include temporary or transient sources (e.g., letters, phone calls, etc.) in its "References" page, preferring to handle them in in-text citations exclusively. This rule holds for electronic sources as well: email, MOOs/MUDs, list server postings, etc., are not included in the "References" page, merely cited in text, for example, "But Wilson has rescinded his earlier support for these policies" (Charles Wilson, personal email to the author, 20 November 1996). But also note that many list server and Usenet groups and MOOs actually archive their correspondences, so that there is a permanent site (usually a Gopher or FTP server) where those documents reside. In that case, you would want to find the archive and cite it as an unchanging source. Strictly speaking, according to the APA manual, a file from an FTP site should be referenced as follows:

```
Deutsch, P. (1991). Archie: An electronic directory
     service for the Internet [Online]. Available
     FTP: ftp.sura.net Directory: pub/archie/docs File:
     whatis.archie.
```

However, the increasing familiarity of Net users with the convention of a URL makes the prose description of how to find a file ("Available FTP: ftp.sura.net Directory: pub/archie/docs File: whatis.archie") unnecessary.

So, with modification of the APA format (as suggested by the APA at its Web page www.apa.org/journals/webref.html), citations from the standard Internet sources would appear as follows.

FTP (File Transfer Protocol) Sites To cite files available for downloading via FTP, give the author's name (if known), the publication date (if available and if different from the date accessed), the full title of the paper (capitalizing only the first word and proper nouns), the date of access, and the address of the FTP site along with the full path necessary to access the file.

Deutsch, P. (1991) Archie: An electronic directory
    service for the Internet. Retrieved January
    25, 2000 from File Transfer Protocol: ftp://
    ftp.sura.net/pub/archie/docs/whatis.archie

WWW Sites (World Wide Web) To cite files available for viewing or downloading via the World Wide Web, give the author's name (if known), the year of publication (if known and if different from the date accessed), the full title of the article, and the title of the complete work (if applicable) in italics. Include any additional information (such as versions, editions, or revisions) in parentheses immediately following the title. Include the date of retrieval and full URL (the http address).

part
3

Burka, L. P. (1993). A hypertext history of multi-
    user dungeons. *MUDdex*. Retrieved January 13, 1997
    from the World Wide Web: http://www.utopia.com/
    talent/lpb/muddex/essay/

Tilton, J. (1995). Composing good HTML (Vers. 2.0.6).
    Retrieved December 1, 1996 from the World Wide Web:
    http://www.cs.cmu.edu/~tilt/cgh/

Synchronous Communications (MOOs, MUDs, IRC, etc.) Give the name of the speaker(s), the complete date of the conversation being referenced in parentheses, and the title of the session (if applicable). Next, list the title of the site in italics, the protocol and address (if applicable), and any directions necessary to access the work. Last, list the date of access, followed by the retrieval information. Personal interviews do not need to be listed in the References, but do need to be included in parenthetic references in the text (see the APA *Publication Manual*).

```
Cross, J. (1996, February 27). Netoric's Tuesday
    cafe: Why use MUDs in the writing classroom?
    MediaMoo. Retrieved March 1, 1996 from
    File Transfer Protocol: ftp://daedalus.com/
    pub/ACW/NETORIC/catalog
```

Gopher Sites List the author's name (if applicable), the year of publication, the title of the file or paper, and the title of the complete work (if applicable). Include any print publication information (if available) followed by the protocol (i.e., gopher://). List the date that the file was accessed and the path necessary to access the file.

```
Massachusetts Higher Education Coordinating Council.
    (1994). Using coordination and collaboration to
    address change. Retrieved July 16, 1999 from
    the World Wide Web: gopher://gopher.mass.edu:170/
    00gopher_root%3A%5B_hecc%5D_plan
```

Email, Listservs, and Newsgroups Do not include personal email in the list of References. Although unretrievable communication such as email is not included in APA References, somewhat more public or accessible Internet postings from newsgroups or listservs may be included. See the APA *Publication Manual* for information on in-text citations.

```
Heilke, J. (1996, May 3). Webfolios. Alliance for
    Computers and Writing Discussion List. Retrieved
    December 31, 1996 from the World Wide Web:
    http://www.ttu.edu/lists/acw-1/9605/0040.html
```

Other authors and educators have proposed similar extensions to the APA style. You can find links to these pages at:

```
www.psychwww.com/resource/apacrib.htm
```

Remember, "frequently-referenced" does not equate to "correct" or even "desirable." Check with your professor to see if your course or school has a preference for an extended APA style.

part
3

Glossary

Your Own Private Glossary

The Glossary in this book contains reference terms you'll find useful as you get started on the Internet. After a while, however, you'll find yourself running across abbreviations, acronyms, and buzzwords whose definitions will make more sense to you once you're no longer a novice (or "newbie"). That's the time to build a glossary of your own. For now, the 2DNet Webopædia gives you a place to start.

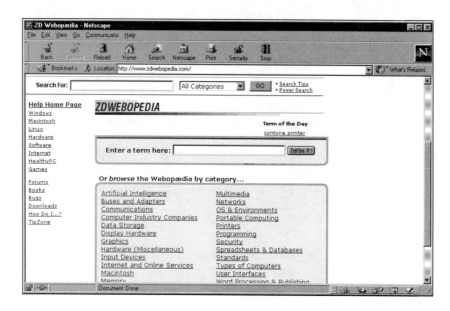

alias
A simple email address that can be used in place of a more complex one.

AVI
Audio Video Interleave. A video compression standard developed for use with Microsoft Windows. Video clips on the World Wide Web are usually available in both AVI and QuickTime formats.

bandwidth
Internet parlance for capacity to carry or transfer information such as email and Web pages.

browser
The computer program that lets you view the contents of Web sites.

client
A program that runs on your personal computer and supplies you with Internet services, such as getting your mail.

cyberspace
The whole universe of information that is available from computer networks. The term was coined by science fiction writer William Gibson in his novel *Neuromancer,* published in 1984.

DNS
See *domain name server.*

domain
A group of computers administered as a single unit, typically belonging to a single organization such as a university or corporation.

domain name
A name that identifies one or more computers belonging to a single domain. For example, "apple.com".

domain name server
A computer that converts domain names into the numeric addresses used on the Internet.

download
Copying a file from another computer to your computer over the Internet.

email

Electronic mail.

emoticon

A guide to the writer's feelings, represented by typed characters, such as the Smiley :-). Helps readers understand the emotions underlying a written message.

FAQs

Frequently Asked Questions

flame

A rude or derogatory message directed as a personal attack against an individual or group.

flame war

An exchange of flames (see above).

FTP

File Transfer Protocol, a method of moving files from one computer to another over the Internet.

home page

A page on the World Wide Web that acts as a starting point for information about a person or organization.

hypertext

Text that contains embedded *links* to other pages of text. Hypertext enables the reader to navigate between pages of related information by following links in the text.

LAN

Local Area Network. A computer network that is located in a concentrated area, such as offices within a building.

link

A reference to a location on the Web that is embedded in the text of the Web page. Links are usually highlighted with a different color or underlined to make them easily visible.

listserv

Strictly speaking, a computer program that administers electronic mailing lists, but also used to denote such lists or discussion groups, as in "the writer's listserv."

lurker

A passive reader of an Internet *newsgroup* or *listserv*. A lurker reads messages, but does not participate in the discussion by posting or responding to messages.

mailing list

A subject-specific automated email system. Users subscribe and receive email from other users about the subject of the list.

modem

A device for connecting two computers over a telephone line.

newbie

A new user of the Internet.

newsgroup

A discussion forum in which all participants can read all messages and public replies between the participants.

plug-in

A third-party software program that will lend a Web browser (Netscape, Internet Explorer, etc.) additional features.

quoted

Text in an email message or newsgroup posting that has been set off by the use of vertical bars or > characters in the left-hand margin.

search engine

A computer program that will locate Web sites or files based on specified criteria.

secure

A Web page whose contents are encrypted when sending or receiving information.

server

A computer program that moves information on request, such as a Web server that sends pages to your browser.

Smiley

See *emoticon.*

snail mail

Mail sent the old fashioned way: Write a letter, put it in an envelope, stick on a stamp, and drop it in the mailbox.

spam

Spam is to the Internet as unsolicited junk mail is to the postal system.

URL

Uniform Resource Locator: The notation for specifying addresses on the World Wide Web (e.g. http://www.abacon.com or ftp://ftp.abacon.com).

Usenet

The section of the Internet devoted to *newsgroups*.

Web browser

A program used to navigate and access information on the World Wide Web. Web browsers convert html coding into a display of pictures, sound, and words.

Web page

All the text, graphics, pictures, and so forth, denoted by a single URL beginning with the identifier "http://".

Web site

A collection of World Wide Web pages, usually consisting of a home page and several other linked pages.